HATE CRIMES

Hal Marcovitz

San Diego, CA

About the Author

A former newspaper reporter and columnist, Hal Marcovitz is the author of nearly two hundred books for young readers. He makes his home in Chalfont, Pennsylvania.

Printed in the United States

For more information, contact:
ReferencePoint Press, Inc.
PO Box 27779
San Diego, CA 92198
www.ReferencePointPress.com

Picture Credits:
Cover: iStockphoto.com

6: Associated Press
10: Maury Aaseng
12: Sipa USA/Associated Press
16: Action Sports Photography/Shutterstock.com
22: Burlingham/Shutterstock.com
27: Associated Press
28: Associated Press
33: Sipa USA/Associated Press
35: Associated Press
38: Associated Press
44: fstop123/iStockphoto.com
47: Jeff Siner/TNS/Newscom
51: Brendan McDermid/Reuters/Newscom
55: Alvarez/iStockphoto.com
60: Susan Montgomery/Shutterstock.com
63: Sipa USA/Associated Press

LIBRARY OF CONGRESS CATALOGING-IN-PUBLICATION DATA

Name: Marcovitz, Hal, author.
Title: Hate Crimes/by Hal Marcovitz.
Description: San Diego, CA: ReferencePoint Press, [2018] | Audience: Grade 9 to 12. | Includes bibliographical references and index.
Identifiers: LCCN 2018021023 (print) | LCCN 2018022042 (ebook) | ISBN 9781682824726 (eBook) | ISBN 9781682824719 (hardback)
Subjects: LCSH: Hate crimes—Juvenile literature. | Offenses against the person—Juvenile literature.
Classification: LCC HV6773.5 (ebook) | LCC HV6773.5 .M367 2018 (print) | DDC 364.15—dc23
LC record available at https://lccn.loc.gov/2018021023

CONTENTS

A Callous Hatred

On the evening of June 17, 2015, a lone man wandered into the Emanuel African Methodist Episcopal Church in Charleston, South Carolina. He took a seat on a pew in the rear of the church. Churchgoers saw nothing unusual in the white man who sat among them as the congregants participated in a Bible study class. Although the church membership is composed of African Americans, the members regarded their congregation as inclusive: anybody who wanted to worship in their church was welcome.

After about forty-five minutes, though, the man suddenly rose to his feet, drew a handgun, and started shooting. Within minutes, nine churchgoers had been murdered. The man who wielded the gun, twenty-one-year-old Dylann Roof, was captured the next day. More than a year later, Roof went on trial for murder. He was convicted and sentenced to the death penalty.

In winning the conviction against Roof, the prosecutor, assistant US attorney Julius Richardson, told jurors, "Little did they know what a cold and hateful heart he had. . . . He hadn't come to the Bible study to hear the good word. He hadn't come to hear the Lord. He chose to execute nine good, innocent men and women. And he chose to do so out of a callous hatred of the color of their skin."[1]

Individuals and Communities Suffer

Roof's act of murder in South Carolina was one of 5,850 hate crimes committed in 2015 in America, according to the Federal Bureau of Investigation (FBI). The nine people who lost their lives that day were among the 7,173 individuals who were victims of hate crimes in 2015. Certainly, the victims murdered that day, as well as members of their families, were among those who suffer the harshest consequences of hate crimes. Other victims typically endure crimes such as vandalism to their homes. Or

> "He chose to execute nine good, innocent men and women. And he chose to do so out of a callous hatred of the color of their skin."[1]
>
> —Federal prosecutor Julius Richardson

they may receive anonymous threatening phone calls. Or they may be physically assaulted, attacked by surprise as they innocently walk down the street.

Regardless of the nature of the harassment, victims often suffer deeply from the crimes that have been committed against them. As Carolyn Turpin-Petrosino, a professor of criminal justice at Bridgewater State University in Massachusetts, explains, "The trauma experienced, both physical and psychological, is more [harmful] than that suffered by victims of comparable non-hate crimes."[2] Simply put, perpetrators of hate crimes wish to send messages to their victims declaring that because of the color of their skin or their ethnicity, religious beliefs, or sexual orientation, they are living where they are not wanted.

Moreover, Turpin-Petrosino points out, victims are not the only people who suffer from the hateful deeds of the perpetrators: whole communities whose members believe themselves to be living in peace and on good terms with their neighbors suddenly find themselves living among people who hate. In February 2018, for example, residents of West Washington Street in Orange, Virginia, found anti-Semitic and racial slurs spray-painted on eight cars parked along the street. Calvin Williams, a fifty-four-year-old resident of Orange, said he had lived in the town his whole life and had never been exposed to the degree of racism found along West Washington Street that morning. "It's crazy," Williams said. "It shouldn't be done. It shouldn't be happening."[3] Orange police chief James Fenwick added, "This is not who we are as a community. This is not something we condone and right now this is our No. 1 priority to find the person or persons responsible and hit them with everything we can."[4]

Bitter Consequences

And yet, despite the shock exhibited by Fenwick and Williams that such a degree of hate could surface in their town, obviously someone who lived in Orange harbored hate toward Jews and African

Americans—and that person resorted to vandalism as a way to express his or her hate. Other perpetrators have chosen much more vicious methods of expressing their hate. Physical assaults have resulted in lasting injuries and—as in the events in Charleston, South Carolina—death. Soon after his arrest, Roof confessed his crimes to the police. He told police he had come to the conclusion that African Americans represented a danger to white people. He also believed that state and federal lawmakers were powerless to stop the violence against white people, so he decided he had no choice—he had to take matters into his own hands. "I had to do it because somebody had to do something," Roof said in the confession. "Black people are killing white people every day on the street, and they are raping white women. What I did is so minuscule to what they're doing to white people every day all the time."[5]

Roof, of course, harbored delusions about the state of race relations in America. In making the decision to commit the mur-

Dylann Roof is escorted from a courthouse in Shelby, North Carolina. In 2015, Roof entered the Emanuel African Methodist church in Charleston, South Carolina, shooting and killing nine African American parishioners.

ders, he had allowed himself to be influenced by the hateful rhetoric of others as well as biased and untrue information he gleaned from the Internet and other sources. Those messages had somehow become hardwired into his brain, causing him to view society through a skewed and hateful prism.

> **"This is not who we are as a community."[4]**
>
> —James Fenwick, the police chief of Orange, Virginia

Soon after his conviction, Roof's attorneys filed appeals, asking for his sentence to be reduced to life imprisonment. As those appeals make their way slowly through the courts, Roof will find himself sitting in his jail cell, watching the days fall away as his execution date grows closer. He will have ample opportunity to ponder the bitter consequences his beliefs have had on his own life as well as the lives of those he took when he planned and carried out his crime of hate.

How Serious a Problem Are Hate Crimes?

Hate crimes may involve vandalism, assault, arson, rape, and even murder. They can be committed by individuals or groups of people. Some hate crimes are planned in advance, and others occur spontaneously. Hate crimes are, therefore, similar to other crimes that are part of the fabric of life during the twenty-first century.

But what sets hate crimes apart from other crimes are the motives behind them. Hate crimes are committed because perpetrators harbor biases against the victims. An ordinary criminal may select a victim because the perpetrator wants to take his or her money or other possessions, such as a car, credit card, or cell phone. In a hate crime, the perpetrator selects a victim because he or she harbors great animosity toward the victim's social group—often African Americans, Hispanic Americans, Jews, Muslims, gays, or others whom the perpetrator has concluded does not belong in society. "The main difference between a hate crime and other crimes is that a perpetrator of a hate crime is motivated by bias," says Nancy Turner, the senior program manager for the Alexandria, Virginia–based International Association of Chiefs of Police. "Hate crimes are unique. Victims of hate crimes are targeted because of a core characteristic of their identity. These attributes cannot be changed. Victims often feel degraded, frightened, vulnerable and suspicious. This may be one of the most traumatic experiences of their lives."[6]

Who Are the Victims?

According to the FBI, there were 6,121 criminal incidents reported in 2016 (the last year for which statistics are available) that were motivated by a bias toward race, ethnicity, ancestry, religion, sexual orientation, disability, gender, or gender identity. In those incidents reported by the FBI, a total of 7,615 people were victimized by hate crimes. Some 58 percent of these incidents were motivated by a bias against the victim's race, ethnicity, or ancestry; 21 percent were motivated by a religious bias; and 18 percent were motivated by a sexual-orientation bias. The remaining incidents were motivated by a gender, gender identity, or disability bias. Meanwhile, officials in Canada reported that in 2016, 1,409 hate crimes were reported in that country—roughly a quarter of the hate crimes committed in the United States. (Canada's population is only about 11 percent as large as the population of the United States.) Of the 1,409 hate crimes reported in Canada, 48 percent were motivated by race or ethnicity. Also, about 33 percent of the crimes were motivated by animosity toward the religious beliefs of the victims, and about 13 percent were motivated by bias against gays. The remaining crimes were motivated by unknown factors, according to Statistics Canada, the government agency that compiles national statistics.

> **"The main difference between a hate crime and other crimes is that a perpetrator of a hate crime is motivated by bias."[6]**
>
> —Nancy Turner, the senior program manager of the International Association of Chiefs of Police

Therefore, in today's world, hate crimes are committed against people because of their religious beliefs, race, or ethnicity; because they are gay or transgender; and even because they have disabilities. In fact, in November 2017 an assailant was sentenced to a prison term of three to six years for sucker punching twenty-two-year-old Michael Patrick Ryan outside a convenience store in West Chester, Pennsylvania. Ryan suffers from cerebral palsy, a disability that often causes patients to walk and otherwise move their limbs with difficulty. As Ryan approached the store, Barry Baker Jr. mocked his gait. Then, as Ryan hobbled by, Baker swung his fist hard, knocking Ryan to the ground.

The incident was caught on a nearby security camera; Baker was arrested and charged with assaulting Ryan. In sentencing

Hate Crimes Committed in 2016

The largest number of hate crimes committed in the United States in 2016 related to race, ethnicity, and ancestry, according to the FBI's most recent compilation of bias-motivated incidents. Religion and sexual orientation represented the next most common categories of hate crimes. FBI statistics are compiled from incident reports submitted by law enforcement agencies around the country.

Bias Incidents by Category, 2016

Single-bias Incidents	
Race/ethnicity/ancestry	3,489
Religion	1,273
Sexual orientation	1,076
Disability	70
Gender	31
Gender identity	124
Multiple-bias Incidents*	**58**
Total	6,121

* A multiple-bias incident is an incident in which one or more offense types are motivated by two or more biases.

Source: FBI, "Hate Crime Statistics, 2016," November 13, 2017. https://ucr.fbi.gov/hate-crime/2016.

Baker, Judge William P. Mahon told the defendant, "You are a bully. You are a predator. You are a coward. In eighteen years on the bench I have never had such tangible evidence of someone's moral compass being so askew."[7]

Who Commits Hate Crimes?

According to experts, Baker could be regarded as the typical perpetrator of a hate crime: he is white, and he was twenty-nine years old at the time he assaulted Ryan. The FBI reports that 46 percent of hate crimes in 2016 were committed by whites, and 26 percent of perpetrators were African American. People of Asian ethnicity committed about 1 percent of the hate crimes, and Native Americans also committed about 1 percent. About 8 percent were committed by groups of individuals of various races. The remaining crimes, about 18 percent, were committed by perpetrators of unknown race or ethnicity.

Experts believe that whites account for most of that 18 percent in the unknown race or ethnicity category, meaning that hate crimes are overwhelmingly committed by whites. Moreover, according to Phyllis B. Gerstenfeld, a psychology professor at the Stanislaus campus of California State University, most perpetrators are males—usually no more than teenagers or, as in Baker's case, young adults. "In recent years, a consistent, if incomplete picture of the 'typical' hate crime offender has emerged," she says. "He is young, white, and male; he does not come from an especially impoverished background [and] he has little or no previous contact with the criminal justice system."[8]

> **"You are a bully. You are a predator. You are a coward. In eighteen years on the bench I have never had such tangible evidence of someone's moral compass being so askew."[7]**
>
> —Pennsylvania judge William P. Mahon

And as the typical offender enters his teen or early adult years, he has learned to hate others. Gerstenfeld points out that very young children do not hate anyone—they play together regardless of race or religion. But over the course of their early years of development, many young people are exposed to hateful environments where they develop their own biases. Perhaps they hear hateful messages from parents or older siblings, find them in the media, or hear complete strangers voice hateful ideas. Regardless of the source, the messages resonate with some young people; over the years these young people are likely to develop their own biases. In many cases, she says, these biases are well developed by the time young people enter middle school. "By then they have adopted society's prejudices, and they will usually reject members of [other groups] behaviorally," she says. "You can verify this by visiting the ethnically diverse middle or high school at lunchtime, where you will see the students mostly sitting with members of their own race or ethnicity."[9]

Hate Groups

As young people develop biases, many of them will seek out others who share their prejudices. It is not hard to find them. Many hate groups maintain presences on the Internet, where they spread their hateful rhetoric. The Ku Klux Klan (KKK), possibly the most notorious of all American hate groups, was established following the end of the Civil War and thc abolition of slavery—both in 1865. Founded by veterans of the Confederate army, the KKK initially directed its venom at losing the war toward the emancipated slaves. The KKK has long since ceased being a national organization, but many small groups continue to claim allegiance to the KKK and have adopted the name and symbols of the Klan. Other groups include versions of so-called neo-Nazis and skinheads, who base their cultures on the National Socialist, or Nazi, movement led by Adolf Hitler in Germany between the 1920s and 1940s. The Nazis orchestrated and carried out events now known as the Holocaust—the persecution and murders of millions of European Jews and others.

A Neo-Nazi gives a speech during a 2018 rally in Newnan, Georgia. Neo-Nazis base their culture on the National Socialist, or Nazi, movement from 1920s–1940s Germany.

Although numerous hate groups exist in modern-day society, most perpetrators of hate crimes are not members of hate groups. The FBI does not keep statistics on how many perpetrators of hate crimes maintain memberships in hate groups, but experts believe these groups are more interested in spreading their hateful messages than in committing actual crimes. In other words, today's typical member of the KKK is more likely to maintain a website, social media presence, or blog to spread the group's racist rhetoric than he or she is to throw a brick through the window of an African American's home.

The Southern Poverty Law Center (SPLC), a civil rights group based in Montgomery, Alabama, estimates that just 5 percent of hate crimes are committed by members of hate groups. In reality, the SPLC says, most hate crimes are committed by so-called lone-wolf perpetrators. But that does not mean hate groups do not play a role in the commission of hate crimes. The SPLC maintains that many perpetrators find inspiration in the messages spread by hate groups: "Many hate crimes are committed by young males acting alone or in small groups, often for thrills. While these perpetrators may act independently, they are sometimes influenced by the dehumanizing rhetoric and propaganda of hate groups."[10]

> **"Many hate crimes are committed by young males acting alone or in small groups, often for thrills. While these perpetrators may act independently, they are sometimes influenced by the dehumanizing rhetoric and propaganda of hate groups."[10]**
>
> —Southern Poverty Law Center

Where Are Hate Crimes Committed?

Whether perpetrators act alone or in small groups, statistics reflect that hate crimes are often committed in specific places. According to FBI statistics, many hate crimes are committed at or near the homes of the victims, suggesting that perpetrators often vandalize the residences or vehicles of the victims. Of the 6,121 incidents reported in 2016, 1,670—or about 27 percent—occurred at or near the homes of the victims.

A typical example could be found in Multnomah County, Oregon. In March 2017, Hasel Afshar arrived home from a three-day vacation out of state to find his Multnomah home had been vandalized with racist graffiti. One of the messages accused Afshar of being an Islamist terrorist. The vandals also left a note at the house, which read, "If I see you here next month, I will shoot you and burn your house."[11]

Afshar said he was so unnerved by the crime that he decided to leave Oregon. He planned to move in with friends either in Canada or Australia. "I'm not going to be a hero and stay here and fight about it," Afshar commented. "I'm not going to sit here and wait for someone to shoot me."[12] Afshar, who was born in Iran, immigrated to America in 2010. Ironically, he is not a Muslim. Instead, he practices the Baha'i faith. Members of the Baha'i faith accept all religions as equal; members seek to live in harmony with all peoples.

> **"I'm not going to be a hero and stay here and fight about it. I'm not going to sit here and wait for someone to shoot me."[12]**
>
> —Oregon hate crime victim Hasel Afshar

The vandalism at Afshar's home actually represented the second racist incident he encountered in Multnomah County. Three weeks earlier, he had parked his car in front of a grocery store. As he stepped out of his car, a white van stopped alongside his vehicle. A man in the van shouted, "Get the [expletive] out of America. We don't want you here."[13]

That incident occurred on a public street—in daylight, in full view of whatever witnesses may have been nearby. In fact, hate crimes are typically committed on public streets. FBI statistics show that 1,128 crimes were committed on public streets in 2016—suggesting to experts that these crimes are usually unplanned. In other words, a perpetrator may see a person walking down the street and makes a spur-of-the-moment decision to commit a hate crime. According to Gerstenfeld, many of these crimes are committed by small groups of perpetrators. Typically, she says, a leader suggests everyone in the group take part in the crime, and others go along. As Gerstenfeld explains, "These [are] cases in which offenders, almost always young and in small

Women Who Commit Hate Crimes

Although the majority of hate crimes are believed to be committed by males, incidents involving female offenders are not uncommon. In December 2017, for example, twenty-nine-year-old Rachel Tuszynski was charged with committing a hate crime, threatening a public official, and criminal damage to property after painting Nazi symbols and other racist graffiti on the home and driveway of Roger Claar, the mayor of Bolingbrook, Illinois. She pleaded guilty and was sentenced to three months in jail.

The FBI does not keep statistics on the gender of known offenders, but a study by another US Justice Department agency, the Bureau of Justice Statistics, found that 17 percent of hate crimes that occurred between 2011 and 2014 were perpetrated by women. Another 8 percent of hate crimes included both male and female perpetrators, the bureau reported.

Carolyn Turpin-Petrosino, a professor of criminal justice at Bridgewater State University in Massachusetts, points out that men who harbor prejudices against others are typically very conservative when it comes to women: They regard women's roles as homemakers, responsible mainly for raising children and cooking meals. And yet, says Turpin-Petrosino, many of these men encourage their wives and girlfriends to commit hate crimes. She says, "It may be disturbing to some to consider that while hate culture primarily supports traditional gender roles for women as homemakers, child rearing, and supporters of their male partners, it also invites them to engage in violent acts."

Carolyn Turpin-Petrosino, *Understanding Hate Crimes: Acts, Motives, Offenders, Victims, and Justice.* New York: Routledge, 2015, p. 117.

groups, are just 'bored and looking for some fun.' In other words, like many young people they [are] looking for a little excitement, only they decided to have it at someone else's expense."[14]

African Americans Are Often Targeted

Very often, the victims of these crimes, whether they are committed by individuals or small groups, are African Americans. As the FBI statistics report, about 58 percent of hate crimes committed in 2016 were attributed to racial or ethnic bias. Of the 4,426 victims in 2016 of this form of bias, 50 percent were African American.

There is no question that African Americans have long suffered bias in American society. First brought to America as slaves in 1619, emancipated during the Civil War, and granted equal rights during the 1960s, African Americans nevertheless continue to suffer from bias well into the twenty-first century. Even the 2008 election of an African American president, Barack Obama, failed to ease many people's prejudices against black people. Gerstenfeld says that "hate crimes continue against African Americans because prejudice continues. Although discrimination and segregation may no longer be legal, they are still commonplace, and many Americans harbor stereotypes of blacks as inferior, dangerous or economically damaging to others."[15]

Hate crimes committed against African Americans can be particularly violent. Among the most notorious cases of the past six decades include the murder of Emmett Till, a fourteen-year-

Even the 2008 election of the first African American president, Barack Obama, failed to ease many people's prejudices against black people. Today, many Americans still view black people as inferior.

old African American who was kidnapped from his home in Mississippi in 1955 and was murdered by two white men. Medgar Evers, a black civil rights activist, was murdered by members of the KKK in 1963. Also in 1963, four young black girls lost their lives when Klan members bombed the Sixteenth Street Baptist Church in Birmingham, Alabama. And in 1968 Martin Luther King Jr., the nation's leading civil rights activist of the era, was assassinated by a white segregationist, James Earl Ray.

Well into the twenty-first century, such violence against African Americans has continued. Indeed, the 2015 murders of nine African American churchgoers in Charleston, South Carolina, stand out as among the most horrific hate crimes in American history.

Targeting Jews

Members of another ethnic group often targeted are people of the Jewish faith. According to the FBI, most hate crimes committed because of religious bias are aimed at Jews. In 2016 the FBI attributed 1,584 hate crimes to religious bias. Fifty-four percent of the victims were Jews.

Jews have been part of American life since colonial times. In 1655 the first Jewish settlers arrived in the colony of New Amsterdam—now New York State. Today some 10 million Jewish adults and children live in America. And yet, even though Jews have been assimilated into American culture for hundreds of years, many still find themselves the targets of anti-Semitism. (The term *anti-Semitism* stems from a prejudice against people who speak the ancient Semitic languages, one of which is Hebrew.) Gerstenfeld cites several reasons for prejudice against Jews. For starters, she points out, even though there are some 10 million Jews living in America, they still make up a tiny portion of the population—just about 3 percent. Therefore, most Americans do not come into contact with Jews on a daily basis and, as such, many may find their beliefs and customs strange and foreign.

Moreover, since there is a long history of anti-Semitism, dating back centuries, Gerstenfeld says that if people find themselves harboring prejudices against Jews it is easy for them to

Hate Crimes in Europe

A study compiled by the European Union (EU) Agency for Fundamental Rights reported a staggeringly high number of hate crimes committed in 2016: more than eighty-three thousand. The EU represents twenty-eight countries in Europe, enabling those countries to work together on economic issues and other common problems, such as human rights. The report by the EU agency looked at hate crimes in seventeen countries.

Although the EU total is considerably higher than statistics recorded in America, EU officials point out that it is difficult to categorize hate crimes in Europe because different countries maintain different notions about what constitutes a hate crime. For example, British law enables prosecutors to bring hate crime cases against perpetrators if victims believe they were targeted because of race, ethnicity, or similar factors. Other countries provide prosecutors with more discretion, enabling them to make that decision. Joanna Goodey, the program manager for the EU Agency for Fundamental Rights, says, "As a reflection of the fact that different countries have experienced and therefore perceive 'hate' crimes differently, there is no single unified definition of hate crime in Europe."

Joanna Goodey and Kauko Aromaa, eds., *Hate Crime*. Helsinki, Finland: European Institute for Crime Prevention and Control, affiliated with the United Nations, 2008, p. 5. www.middlebury.edu.

find bold and hateful claims about Jews made in the past. A simple Internet search can easily turn up hateful rhetoric about Jews dating back to ancient Roman times. And finally, Gerstenfeld explains, many people perceive Jews as wielding considerable power and influence over American commerce and government—a factor that has led to resentment against Jews. She says, "Hate groups hate a great many people, but the group they have the greatest fear of is Jews because people of that group are presumed to have the power to carry out their nefarious plans."[16]

One recent hate crime perpetrated against Jews occurred in Philadelphia, Pennsylvania, in February 2017: Perpetrators entered a Jewish cemetery and vandalized some five hundred headstones. "I'm a child of a Holocaust survivor so I grew up with stories of destruction of Jewish cemeteries," says Rebecka

Hess, a Philadelphia woman who volunteered to help clean up the cemetery after the vandalism. "I always thought we were done with that."[17]

Anyone May Be a Victim

Although the majority of hate crimes based on religious bias are committed against Jews, in recent years Muslims have increasingly become targets as well. In 2016 the FBI reported 307 hate crimes against members of the Islamic faith, or about 25 percent of the crimes committed on the basis of religious bias. A decade earlier the FBI reported 156 hate crimes against Muslims, which accounted for about 10 percent of hate crimes based on religious bias committed in 2006.

Clearly, many Muslims in America find themselves victims of prejudices that first surfaced following the 2001 Islamist terrorist attacks that took the lives of some three thousand people in New York City; Washington, DC; and Shanksville, Pennsylvania. "The bigot equates Islam with terrorism," says Professor Carolyn Turpin-Petrosino. "Victims of anti-Muslim-motivated hate crimes are innocent victims, undeserving of this infliction."[18]

But it is just not African Americans, Jews, and Muslims who are the targets of hate crimes. Included in the FBI statistics are incidents targeting Catholics, Protestants, Jehovah's Witnesses, Sikhs, Mormons, Hindus, and Buddhists. White people, Hispanic Americans, and Native Americans have been targeted. So have gays and transgender people as well as disabled people. In America, as well as in many other countries, hate crimes are committed every day. Virtually anyone may become a victim.

How Are People Hurt by Hate Crimes?

Ben Stoviak and Aaron MacLachlan, two gay men living in the Lawrenceville neighborhood of Pittsburgh, Pennsylvania, left a bar one evening in 2013, intending to return to their home. While walking to their car, the couple was approached by three men, who taunted them with gay slurs. At first, Stoviak and MacLachlan ignored the comments and walked on, but the three men quickly caught up to the couple and surrounded them. Suddenly, one of the men punched Stoviak, knocking him to the ground. The three men then continued the assault on Stoviak, punching and kicking him several times. After pummeling Stoviak for a few minutes, the three men got into a car and left.

Witnesses summoned police. When the officers arrived, they found Stoviak suffering numerous bruises and bleeding wounds. His attackers also broke two of his teeth. MacLachlan was assaulted during the incident as well but escaped uninjured. Ultimately, police were able to track down one of the perpetrators—a witness took down his vehicle license plate number. The attacker eventually pleaded guilty to assault and received a sentence of three months on probation, meaning he did not have to serve time in prison. The other two assailants were never charged.

The attack sent shock waves through Pittsburgh's gay community. "It makes me sick to my stomach. I feel rage," said Andrew Henderson, a friend of Stoviak's. "It's just sad. It's really sad. We just can't be who we are in our own neighborhood."[19]

A Form of Terrorism

The attack on Stoviak and MacLachlan illustrates how hate crimes affect more than just the victims. A week after the attack on the two men, hundreds of gay residents of Lawrenceville, as well as others, staged a rally to show support for Stoviak and MacLachlan and to denounce prejudice. "This really is a hate crime," said Angela Suroviec, who attended the rally. "I know I live myself in fear for expressing affection. So, for example, if I go to the movies with my girlfriend, you'd want to hold your partner's hand, but I don't do that because I'm afraid someone would hurt me in some significant way."[20]

> **"If I go to the movies with my girlfriend, you'd want to hold your partner's hand, but I don't do that because I'm afraid someone would hurt me in some significant way."[20]**
>
> —Angela Suroviec, a gay resident of Pittsburgh

Studies have found that hate crimes committed against gay people can often have a ripple effect on the local gay community, causing many members to feel unsafe and psychologically damaged. A 2008 study by Kansas State University found that

> the brutality of hate crimes has consequences for the entire community, not just the victim. It is not an exaggeration to say that bias-motivated attacks function as a form of terrorism, sending a message to all lesbians and gay men that they are not safe if they are visible. Thus, when even one does not personally know the victim, hate crimes can threaten the illusion of invulnerability that is so important to one's daily life.[21]

Stoviak was able to recover quickly from his injuries—he addressed the crowd at the Lawrenceville rally. Other gay victims of hate crime attacks have not been as fortunate. The Kansas State University report said physical assaults on gay men are among the most vicious incidents investigated by police. The report quoted a hospital official in New York City who said, "Attacks against gay men were the most heinous and brutal I encountered. . . . They

Same-sex couples often feel unsafe displaying affection in public. They fear that those harboring resentment toward gay people might harass or harm them.

frequently involve torture, cutting, mutilations . . . showing the absolute intent to rub out the human being because of his (sexual) preference."[22]

Psychological Damage Lingers

Even if victims like Stoviak are able to quickly recover from their physical wounds, the psychological damage can linger. "A gay or lesbian person who encounters an expression of hostility because of his or her sexual orientation does not know in advance how the incident will end," explains the Kansas State University report. "He or she may be attacked with words or a deadly weapon. . . . An incident that appears minor in retrospect might nevertheless have considerable psychological consequences on the victim."[23]

Other victims of bias also find themselves enduring mental anguish years after their initial wounds heal. Two years after he was attacked by a man wielding a knife, Steven Woodson, an African American, says he still suffers from deep psychological trauma.

The incident occurred in March 2016 outside an Orlando, Florida, apartment building where a friend of Woodson's lives. Woodson had been visiting his friend; the two men were sitting on a bench in front of the building when fifty-seven-year-old Joel Hunt approached them. Hunt told the two men he lived in the building. He told them he did not like African Americans and ordered them to leave.

Woodson said that he and his friend did not want to get into an altercation with Hunt, so they began walking away. But Hunt became enraged and followed after Woodson and his friend, shouting racial slurs at them. Suddenly, Hunt lunged at Woodson, stabbing him in the stomach.

Woodson tried to escape. He stumbled away from Hunt, holding his hand over his bleeding stomach. Hunt continued to follow him, shouting that he intended to kill Woodson. "He could have killed me and took me away from my mother and father, my two kids, and they would have been without a father," Woodson says. "I could have been gone, because that was his intention—to kill me."[24]

Police were summoned. Woodson was hospitalized. Although treated for his injuries, Woodson has never fully recovered. The knife cut into Woodson's liver, and he has had to endure complications from the injury. He has lost twenty pounds since the attack and has been unable to return to work.

> **"I built this wall and shell around me and stayed away from people. My friends came around and they tried to get me out and go places with them, and I wouldn't go."[25]**
>
> **—Steven Woodson, a hate crime victim in Orlando, Florida**

But the most difficult part of his recovery, he says, has been the psychological trauma. Woodson says he became a shut-in, too fearful of the outside world to leave his home. "I built this wall and shell around me and stayed away from people," Woodson explains. "And my friends came around and they tried to get me out and go places with them, and I wouldn't go. But I think now I'm coming out of it a little more."[25]

As for Hunt, he was convicted in the assault on Woodson. By early 2018 Hunt had not yet been sentenced. He faces up to thirty years in prison.

Hate: A Public Health Concern

The rise in the number of hate crimes, as well as the incendiary rhetoric often voiced by hate groups, has given public health officials cause for concern. They warn about the effects on public health of discrimination and hatred—and crimes committed as a result of hatred.

A 2015 report by the American Psychological Association found that 61 percent of American adults have experienced a degree of hate during their lives. Most of these cases do not rise to the severity of hate crimes, the report said, but could include racial slurs by others or a belief that they have been discriminated against—such as being turned down for a job because of their race or ethnicity. A person who believes they are a victim of bias may feel stress, the association states, which could lead to physical and mental illnesses.

As the medical journal *Modern Healthcare* reports,

> Evidence has shown stress caused by discrimination has been associated with poorer health outcomes, resulting in health disparities between populations that are victims of discrimination and those that are not. A 2014 study . . . found a greater likelihood of suicide among [gay and transgender] public school students who lived in neighborhoods in Boston where there was a higher prevalence of hate crimes targeting those populations. Other research has shown hate crime victims are at higher risk of developing long-term behavioral health disorders such as depression and anxiety as a result of their trauma.

Steven Ross Johnson, "Experts: Hate Crimes Are a Public Health Issue," *Modern Healthcare*, August 22, 2017. www.modernhealthcare.com.

Permanently Disabled

Hate crime victims like Woodson find they have to overcome tremendous psychological trauma to return to their normal lives. Many victims not only have to cope with psychological trauma but also permanent physical disabilities. Although the FBI does not keep statistics on the severity of the injuries sustained by hate crime victims, the agency's 2016 report said a total of 2,560 victims were physically assaulted—suggesting that many of those victims are likely to have sustained injuries.

Among the victims who have sustained debilitating injuries is Kimball Hartman, a twenty-nine-year-old transgender woman who suffered permanent brain damage during an assault on a New York City street in October 2014. She was attacked by an assailant who struck her in the back of the head with a large piece of plexiglass.

Hartman and a gay friend were walking along the street when they were approached by twenty-six-year-old Mashawn Sonds, who shouted antigay slurs at them. As Hartman and her friend started to run away, Sonds hurled the plexiglass at her, striking her in the back of the head. She immediately collapsed and lost consciousness. When an ambulance crew arrived, they found Hartman bleeding from head wounds. In January 2016, Sonds was convicted in the assault and was sentenced to twenty years in prison.

Sixteen months after the assault, Hartman was still too incapacitated to attend the trial and sentencing. She wrote a victim impact statement, though, which was read in court before the judge pronounced the sentence on Sonds. "I may never have the opportunity to live like I used to again because of someone's hate," Hartman's statement said. "[I have lost] my independence possibly forever."[26]

Others have faced similar circumstances. Jack Price, a forty-nine-year-old gay man, was assaulted by two perpetrators on a New York City street in 2009. During the assault, Price sustained a broken jaw, several broken ribs, two collapsed lungs, and a lacerated spleen. Price was attacked as he exited a delicatessen in the New York borough of Queens. The two assailants, twenty-six-year-old Daniel Aleman and twenty-one-year-old Daniel Rodriguez, both from New York City, shouted gay slurs at Price before assaulting him. They also robbed Price, stealing his wallet. Both men were apprehended; Rodriguez was sentenced to twelve years in prison, and Aleman received eight years. "Hate crimes such as this will not be tolerated here in Queens,"[27] said District Attorney Richard Brown.

Following his release from the hospital, Price was unable to return to his job. He has also required the use of a cane to walk.

After the two men were sentenced, Price commented, "I didn't deserve this. I cannot understand how anyone could hate me or anybody else this much to cause him this much pain and suffering. It shows how much hate they have inside of them."[28]

Hate-Fueled Killings

There are times when hatred reaches an even more dangerous level—resulting in loss of life. Nine people were murdered by individuals who committed hate crimes in 2016, according to FBI statistics.

Srinivas Kuchibhotla was killed in a hate crime committed in 2017 in Kansas. Kuchibhotla and his wife, Sunayana Dumala, both arrived in America during the mid-2000s to attend college as engineering students. Both were born in India. After graduation they married and remained in America, finding a home in Olathe, Kansas, a suburb of Kansas City. Kuchibhotla found a job as an aviation engineer; his wife joined the information technology department of a pharmaceutical marketing company.

> **"I cannot understand how anyone could hate me or anybody else this much to cause him this much pain and suffering. It shows how much hate they have inside of them."[28]**
>
> **—Jack Price, a New York City hate crime victim**

In February 2017, thirty-two-year-old Kuchibhotla and a friend stopped at a restaurant on the way home from work for drinks. While at the bar, the two friends were approached by Adam Purinton. "Out of the blue comes this weird-looking gentleman, I say weird-looking because he had anger on his face," recalled Kuchibhotla's friend, Alok Madasani. "I did not hear what he was saying instantly, but I saw the look on Srinivas's face change drastically. I looked at Adam and he walked towards me, he came to me and said, 'Are you here legally?'"[29]

Purinton accused the two men of being from Iran, a majority-Muslim country that has had tense relations with America for more than forty years. Other people in the restaurant said they heard Purinton shout, "Get out of my country."[30] The two men tried to

Relatives grieve around the body of Srinivas Kuchibhotla. Kuchibhotla was murdered by a racist white man at a restaurant in a suburb of Kansas City.

ignore Purinton, who continued to harass them. Finally, Kuchibhotla left the bar to find the restaurant manager, who asked Purinton to leave the building.

Purinton left the restaurant but returned minutes later. He approached the bar, pointed a gun at Kuchibhotla and Madasani, and fired. Kuchibhotla was struck first; he collapsed to the floor. Madasani dove under a table. “All I was thinking about at the time was my baby, all I was thinking of was my wife’s belly,” said Madasani, whose wife was pregnant with their first child at the time. “In flashes, I was thinking, ‘I have to live.’”[31]

Kuchibhotla had been hit in the chest; his wound proved fatal. Madasani was struck in the leg. A third man, Ian Grillot, who attempted to intervene, was struck by gunfire in the hand, neck, and chest; miraculously, he survived. Purinton fled from the scene but was later apprehended. In March 2018 he pleaded guilty to the murder of Kuchibhotla and attempted murders of Madasani and Grillot; he received a sentence of life in prison.

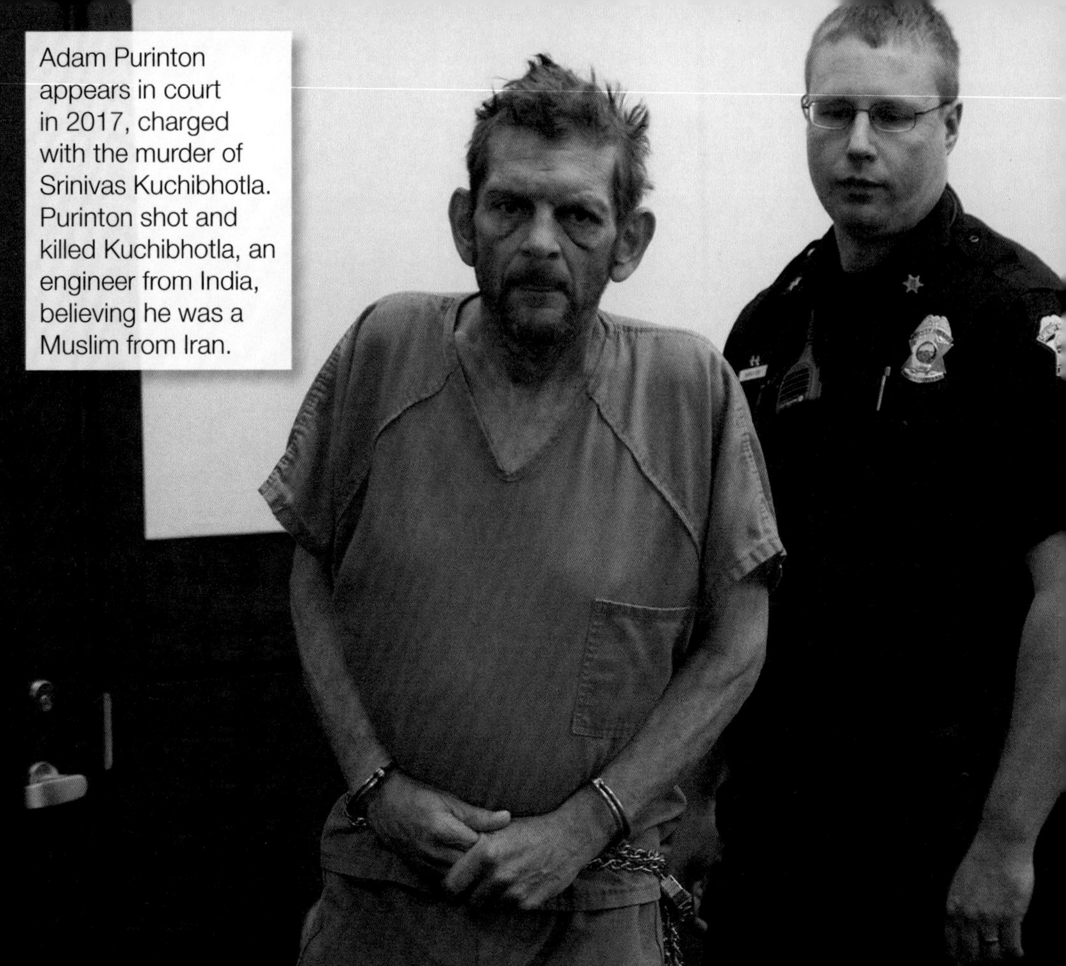
Adam Purinton appears in court in 2017, charged with the murder of Srinivas Kuchibhotla. Purinton shot and killed Kuchibhotla, an engineer from India, believing he was a Muslim from Iran.

Although Purinton will spend the rest of his life in prison, Dumala will spend the rest of her life without her husband, whom she called "Srinu." She says, "What should I do? What is this life? Is it true that I cannot see Srinu? Is it true that I can't hear his voice? Is it true I lost the person who loves me the most?" Months after her husband's death, Dumala stopped at a grocery store in Olathe where she and Kuchibhotla often shopped together. She paused at an open bin of eggplants and sighed deeply. "This was his favorite food," she said. "It didn't matter how you cooked them, he loved any recipe made with eggplant."[32]

The Descent into Hopelessness

Many of those who experience the ugliness of hate crimes eventually recover. Some do not. Trevor O'Brien had, for years, endured gay slurs and bullying from classmates and others in his hometown of Gillette, Wyoming. When O'Brien was in high school, teachers often invited him to sit with them at lunch to ensure he would not be bullied in the school cafeteria. After he graduated and found a job, the gay slurs and bullying continued. During one incident, O'Brien had parked his car in front of a convenience store, which he then entered. A few minutes later he emerged from the store to find a gay slur scratched into the paint of his car. In fact, it was the second time O'Brien's car had been vandalized. "I know that really bothered him," said a friend, Brandi Means. "He said that it made him cry, and he was embarrassed."[33]

In December 2015 O'Brien attended a party. As he left the party, he was approached by five men. The men shouted gay slurs at O'Brien. He attempted to shrug them off, but then they attacked him. He was punched, kicked, and thrown to the ground. During

The Financial Cost of Hate Crimes

Victims of hate crimes often not only have to endure physical injuries and emotional pain but also financial stress. Arriving home one evening in 2017, sixty-three-year-old Kanwal Khurana heard someone shout "Go back to your own country." The next day, the immigrant from India now living in Cleveland, Ohio, discovered all four tires on his car had been slashed.

Khurana, a retired county government employee, called the police, but without witnesses or other evidence there was little they could do to track down the perpetrators. Ultimately, it cost Khurana $500 to have his car towed to a repair shop and four new tires installed.

Under Ohio law Khurana would have been entitled to restitution from the perpetrators—if police had been able to find them. The Ohio state government does, however, maintain a fund to help victims recover from crimes—but only if they sustain physical injuries. Ultimately, Khurana's wife was forced to sell some of her jewelry to pay for the new tires.

Still, Khurana says he feels fortunate that just his car was vandalized. He fears that he could very well have been assaulted and injured. "That night anything could have happened," he says. "We still feel lucky."

Quoted in Anna North, "After Hate Crimes, Victims Get Stuck with the Bill," *New York Times*, April 26, 2017. www.nytimes.com.

the assault O'Brien was kicked in the groin so hard that for days after the attack he found it difficult to urinate. After the party he limped home and refused to call the police, believing they would have little sympathy for him. "I begged him to let me call the cops and he said, 'If you call the cops I'll never forgive you,'"[34] said a friend, Rhonda Pederson.

But O'Brien seemed to change after that night. Prior to the assault, he had usually been able to shrug off the bullying and taunts. After the attack, though, friends and family members say he grew quiet and withdrawn—he was clearly depressed. Finally, on March 7, 2016, O'Brien did not return home after work. He was found dead the next day in a Gillette park. Trevor O'Brien, just twenty years old, had killed himself.

Hate crimes, no matter what form they take, leave no victims unscathed. When an individual is subjected to an act of hatred, he or she may experience short-term anger and fear, enduring pain, or lasting loss. The same can be said for family and friends—and even whole neighborhoods and communities. Whatever the response, the hurt caused by hate crimes is undeniable.

How Do Laws Address Hate Crimes?

As a member of the Sikh faith, Maan Singh Khalsa follows the tenets of his religion very closely. He wears a turban, refrains from shaving or having his hair cut, and often dresses in the traditional robes associated with Sikhism. Most Sikhs live in India, but many have immigrated to other countries. Khalsa settled in Richmond, California, where he works as an information technology specialist.

On September 25, 2016, Khalsa was driving home from work when a pickup truck carrying five men pulled alongside his car. As he waited at a red light, the occupants of the truck hurled empty beer cans at him. When the light changed, Khalsa sped away, but the truck followed his car. When he was forced to stop at the next red light, two men—thirty-one-year-old Chase Little and twenty-five-year-old Colton Leblanc—got out of the truck and assaulted Khalsa. They punched him in the face through his open car window. They knocked off his turban and, using a knife, cut off some of his hair. Khalsa sustained numerous bruises to his face as well as damage to his teeth. He was also wounded in the finger by the knife attack—later, the finger had to be amputated due to an infection. "Cutting a Sikh's hair is one of the most humiliating things anyone can do to a Sikh," Khalsa said later. "By cutting my hair, the attackers did not just attack my body; they attacked my dignity, my spirit, my faith, my religion and my entire community."[35]

Little and Leblanc were apprehended by police, who suggested the perpetrators may have thought they were attacking a Muslim. Both men were charged under a 1987 California law that makes it a crime to assault an individual because of a bias against disability, gender, nationality, race, ethnicity, religion, or sexual orientation.

In May 2017 Little and Leblanc pleaded guilty to the assault on Khalsa under the California hate crimes statute. Both men were sentenced to three years in prison—the harshest penalty available under California law. Had they been convicted in an assault that was not based on bias, they could have faced much lighter sentences. "The attack upon Mr. Khalsa based upon his perceived religion and identity is an attack upon us all," argued Simon O'Connell, the district attorney of Contra Costa County in California, who prosecuted the two defendants. "As a community we must do better and it is my hope that today's sentence moves us further in that direction."[36]

Roadblocks in Five States

California was among the first states to enact a hate crime law, defining offenses regarded as hate crimes as well as the types of bias that are covered under the law. This happened during the 1980s. Laws differ from state to state on what crimes can be considered crimes of hate as well as who is protected under the laws. Even so, essentially all hate crime laws serve the same purpose: they enhance the penalties that can be levied on individuals convicted of committing crimes based on bias. "The burning of a cross in front of a mixed race family's home, the painting of a swastika on the front door of a Jewish synagogue, the physical assault of gays and lesbians, the knifing of a black man by two white men wearing hoods, are all examples of incidents which have happened in Maine in the recent past," wrote Maine attorney general Michael Carpenter in 1992, a year before the Maine legislature passed the state's first hate crime law. "Such conduct cannot and will not be tolerated in this state. Hate crimes are enormously destructive to the victims and, furthermore, are destructive to our society as a whole."[37]

By 2018, forty-five states had enacted their own versions of hate crime laws. The five states without such laws are Georgia, Wyoming, South Carolina, Indiana, and Arkansas. Some lawmakers in those states have made attempts to write hate crime bills, but they have been unable to gain the support they need for adoption. In Indiana, for example, a hate crime bill failed to garner enough votes for passage in 2018. One of the roadblocks

Headstones at this Jewish cemetery were vandalized in 2017. Forty-five states in the United States have enacted hate crime laws that enhance penalties for individuals convicted of crimes based on bias.

against the bill's adoption was its inclusion of protections for gay and transgender people.

Several lawmakers in Indiana oppose granting gay and transgender citizens any protections above those reserved for all citizens, such as the right for transgender citizens to use public bathrooms appropriate for their gender identity. Therefore, those lawmakers would not agree to include gay and transgender people in the protections under the hate crimes bill, causing the bill to die for lack of votes. According to Curt Smith, president of the Indiana Family Institute, a group that opposes the expansion of rights for gay and transgender people, providing special protections for those citizens under the state criminal code helps legitimize the gay and transgender movement. "Why is the Indiana General Assembly again debating so-called 'hate-crimes' legislation?" says Smith. "The short answer is the [gay and transgender] community seeks to politicize the criminal code to elevate its legal status."[38]

But Indiana state senator Susan Glick, who wrote the hate crime bill, insists that all Indianans—including gay and transgender people—need to find protections from hate crimes in state law. Glick, a former prosecutor in LaGrange County, Indiana, says, "When it comes to hate, when it comes to bias, I think it's very important that we protect all of our citizens."[39]

McKinney's Life Is Spared by the Shepards

After he was charged in the 1998 murder of Matthew Shepard, Russell Henderson agreed to plead guilty. In exchange for the plea, prosecutors agreed not to seek the death penalty against him, and the defendant was sentenced to life imprisonment. But Henderson's codefendant, Aaron McKinney, insisted on his innocence and went on trial. McKinney was convicted after a ten-day trial in 1999.

Before the sentencing phase of the trial commenced—when jurors would be asked by prosecutors to condemn McKinney to death—the trial suddenly halted. Shepard's parents, Dennis and Judy Shepard, asked Judge Barton Voigt to dismiss the jury and sentence McKinney to life in prison. Facing McKinney in the courtroom, Dennis Shepard said, "I would like nothing better than to see you die, Mr. McKinney. However, this is the time to begin the healing process. To show mercy to someone who refused to show any mercy. Mr. McKinney, I am going to grant you life, as hard as it is for me to do so, because of Matthew."

Dennis Shepard said the couple asked the judge to spare McKinney's life because Matthew had been a forgiving person who often helped others. Prosecutors told Voigt they had no objections to a term of life imprisonment for McKinney. The judge then passed that sentence—sending McKinney to jail for the rest of his life. Prosecutor Cal Rerucha remarked, "I will never get over Judy Shepard's capacity to forgive."

Quoted in Julie Cart, "Killer of Gay Student Is Spared Death Penalty," *Los Angeles Times*, November 5, 1999. http://articles.latimes.com.

Existing Laws Are Sufficient

Another state lacking its own hate crime law is Wyoming. According to FBI statistics, few hate crimes occur in the state. In 2016 police agencies reported just three hate crimes committed in Wyoming. A year earlier, two hate crimes were reported in the state. In 2014 police in Wyoming reported no hate crimes.

Wyoming's lack of a hate crime law has been challenged by many activists in the state, including the uncle of a Native American man whose violent death was not considered a hate crime by prosecutors. The murder was committed by Roy Clyde, a thirty-two-year-old employee of the parks department of Riverton, Wyoming. Over the years, Clyde grew to harbor animosity toward homeless people whom he saw sleeping, urinating, and defecating in city parks. In July 2015 Clyde approached two men he believed to be homeless, Stallone Trosper and James Goggles, shooting both victims at close range. Neither man was homeless, but both were Native Americans. Trosper died in the attack; Goggles sustained a gunshot wound but survived.

A year after the shooting, Clyde was sentenced to life in prison for the murder of Trosper and attempted murder of Goggles. Speaking during Clyde's sentencing, Trosper's uncle, James Trosper, said that although Clyde may have insisted he targeted homeless people, the real source of his bias should have been obvious. "That same prejudice that we believe killed Stallone still exists today," said Trosper. "It's what my mother experienced when she was a little girl and she would see those signs that said, 'No Indians and no dogs allowed.' It exists today. We can't just leave it in the past and just forget about it. We need to work on it, so that we can get

James Trosper speaks with reporters outside a courthouse in Lander, Wyoming. Trosper believes that the murder of his Native American nephew, Stallone Trosper, was a hate crime.

rid of the prejudice that exists and there can be an understanding between our communities."[40]

Still, the harshness of the sentence handed down to Clyde—life imprisonment—would seem to support the reason why many of Wyoming's political leaders oppose implementation of a hate crime law. They contend the state's existing laws are sufficient to protect all citizens, regardless of the color of their skin or their ethnicity, religious affiliation, or gender identity. "You don't get to shoot somebody and get a pass because it wasn't proven as a hate crime," insists Wyoming governor Matt Mead. "I don't believe I know of a case in Wyoming where there's been a failure of prosecution or a failure of opportunity to seek justice because of a lack of laws for the state."[41]

> **"You don't get to shoot somebody and get a pass because it wasn't proven as a hate crime."[41]**
>
> —Wyoming governor Matt Mead

Incidents in Wyoming and Texas

Nevertheless, there are many advocates for hate crime legislation in Wyoming, and they intend to pursue their cause. "It's short-sighted and doesn't recognize the problem that hate crimes are different than other crimes," says Bruce Palmer, a leader of the Democratic Party in Fremont County, Wyoming, which includes the town of Riverton. "Not only is the direct victim victimized, the community is victimized by them. In the wake of the Riverton incident, I have heard from Native American families who are concerned about going into Riverton that something could happen to them."[42]

Supporters of hate crime legislation in Wyoming point out that it was an incident in Wyoming, as well as a second incident in Texas, that helped galvanize a national recognition of the harms caused by hate crimes, leading to the adoption of a federal hate crime law. "Two horrific murders took place that changed the way hate crime is treated in the American criminal justice system. . . . Both vicious attacks spawned nationwide debates about hate crimes, racism, and homophobia," comments Meredith Worthen, a professor of sociology at the University of Oklahoma. "Both [victims] experienced oppression for who they were and their lives will forever be connected as a result of their gruesome and violent bias-related murders and the outpouring of support and activism following their deaths."[43]

The law, adopted by Congress in 2009, is named the Matthew Shepard and James Byrd Jr. Hate Crimes Prevention Act. It is named for two victims of hate crimes—Matthew Shepard, a gay man who was murdered near Laramie, Wyoming, and James Byrd Jr., an African American man murdered in Jasper, Texas. Both murders were committed in 1998.

Two Gruesome Murders

Both cases are regarded as particularly gruesome. On the night of October 6, 1998, Shepard, a college student, met two men at a bar in Laramie. The perpetrators, Aaron McKinney and Russell Henderson, told Shepard they would give him a ride home. Instead, they drove him to a remote field near Laramie, where they pistol-whipped Shepard, robbed him, took his shoes, and tied him to a fence post, leaving him to die with a fractured skull. A day later, a bicyclist discovered Shepard—he was still alive but in a coma. Shepard died six days later in a Colorado hospital.

McKinney and Henderson were arrested the same night as the assault on Shepard. After leaving Shepard in the field, they returned to Laramie, where they picked a fight with two Hispanic men. Police broke up the fight but suspected McKinney and Henderson were involved in something more sinister; while inspecting McKinney's truck they found a blood-stained gun and Shepard's shoes and credit card. "I think a lot of gay people, when they first heard of that horrifying event, felt sort of punched in the stomach," says gay rights advocate Andrew Sullivan. "I mean it kind of encapsulated all our fears of being victimized."[44] Henderson pleaded guilty to the murder, and McKinney was convicted after a trial by jury. Both men were sentenced to life in prison.

The murder of Byrd occurred on June 7, 1998. He was assaulted and kidnapped by three white supremacists—Shawn Berry, Lawrence Russell Brewer, and John King—in Jasper,

In 1998, James Byrd Jr., who was African American, was chained to a pickup truck by white supremacists and dragged for three miles to his death. An attorney prosecuting the case displays the chain used in the crime.

Texas. They tied him to the back of a truck and then drove for 3 miles (5 km), dragging Byrd behind over an asphalt road. He is believed to have been alive for most of the ordeal, but he died when his body struck a concrete pipe alongside the road. The perpetrators continued on, dumping his body at a cemetery in Jasper. All three men were convicted in the murder. Berry was sentenced to life imprisonment; Brewer and King were sentenced to death. Brewer was executed in 2011; as of May 2018, King remained on death row in a Texas prison, awaiting his execution date.

The National Conversation About Hate Crime

The murders of Shepard and Byrd sparked a national conversation about hate crimes. Professor Carolyn Turpin-Petrosino observes, "Both James Byrd Jr. and Matthew Shepard were brutally murdered in 1998, in different areas of the country, due to their race and sexual orientation. . . . These deaths triggered public outrage; each brought public demonstrations and marches that vowed to bring pressure to legislatures to pass laws to stem these types of tragic crimes."[45]

Advocates for the rights of gays, African Americans, and others held rallies in several cities. At a November 1999 rally in New York City, Ed Sedarbaum, the associate director of the New York regional office of the Anti-Defamation League, a Jewish civil rights group, pointed out that people who commit hate crimes are often first-time offenders; therefore, in states lacking hate crime laws, they often receive leniency from prosecutors and judges. "We are convinced that the creation of harsher penalties [for hate crimes] makes sense because, in fact, very often the perpetrators of violent bias crimes are first-time offenders, so very often they end up being out on probation. So the message ends up being: 'We don't take this kind of crime very seriously,' be it assault or aggravated harassment."[46]

Despite the public activism, it took supporters in Congress eleven years following the deaths of Shepard and Byrd to muster enough votes to pass the law. Finally, on October 28, 2009, President Obama signed the Matthew Shepard and James Byrd Jr. Hate Crimes Prevention Act into law.

Shepard-Byrd Act Expands Protections

In addition to the Shepard-Byrd act, Congress has taken other steps to categorize certain crimes as hate crimes. As far back as 1968 Congress passed a law making it illegal to use violence or intimidation to deny a US citizen the right to vote, attend public school, serve on a jury, or participate in other civil rights because of race, ethnicity, or gender. Vandalizing places of worship was declared a federal crime under an act passed in 1996. And a 2009 federal law prohibits using violence or intimidation to deny housing to people because of race, ethnicity, or gender.

The Shepard-Byrd act expanded federal protections to people for just being themselves—making it a federal crime to, for example, assault a gay man on the street or vandalize the home of an African American. Prior to adoption of the Shepard-Byrd act, such offenses were regarded as lesser local crimes. Moreover, in states lacking their own hate crime laws, federal prosecutors now had the authority to step in and charge the perpetrators with crimes based on bias.

Moreover, the Shepard-Byrd act is comprehensive, protecting every known category of bias. Likewise, the federal law imposes

Should Hate Speech Be a Hate Crime?

In October 2017, a flyer posted on a bulletin board at Cleveland State University in Ohio urging gay and transgender people to take their own lives. When the flyers were discovered, school officials immediately had them removed. They later acknowledged that whoever posted the flyers had broken no laws. "While I find the message of this poster reprehensible, the current legal framework regarding free speech makes it difficult to prevent these messages from being disseminated," explained university president Ronald Berkman.

Similarly, a person who stands outside a synagogue, on a public sidewalk, handing out leaflets proclaiming anti-Semitic messages is well within his or her rights under the First Amendment to the US Constitution, which protects free speech. However, if that person paints a swastika on the door of a synagogue, that act would be regarded as a criminal offense under hate crime statutes in many states as well as federal law. By painting the image on the door, the perpetrator commits an act of vandalism that qualifies as a hate crime. "If you are beating somebody up, obviously you can be charged with a hate crime if you're doing that with the intention of targeting them because of their race," says Margaret Russell, a professor of law at Santa Clara University in California. "But if you're walking beside that person on the sidewalk with a sign or handing out fliers that reflect hatred toward that race, that is protected."

Quoted in Karen Farkas, "Flier at Cleveland State University Encouraging LGBTQ Students to Consider Suicide Upsets Students," Cleveland.com, October 17, 2017. www.cleveland.com.

Quoted in Jeremy Hobson, "Why Hate Speech Is Protected Under the Law," *Here and Now*, NPR, February 20, 2017. www.wbur.org.

much harsher penalties on cases involving bias than many of the state or local laws. For example, under the federal hate crime statute, a conviction for committing a hate crime with a gun brings an automatic sentence of ten years in prison. Also, a maximum penalty of death is imposed by the federal law for crimes that result in the death of the victim. This component of the law gives federal prosecutors the authority to seek the death penalty even in states where it is not normally permitted. By 2018, twenty-two states did not permit the death penalty for murder convictions—but in those states, perpetrators can be executed if they are convicted under the federal hate crime law.

A Need for Continuing Dialogue

The first defendants charged and convicted under the Shepard-Byrd Act were twenty-year-old Frankie Maybee and nineteen-year-old Sean Popejoy, both of Green Forest, Arkansas—a state lacking its own hate crime law. According to prosecutors, in 2011 Maybee and Popejoy approached five Hispanic men at a gas station. They shouted racial slurs at the five men. The victims tried to drive away but were pursued by Maybee and Popejoy, who rammed their truck into the victims' car. The collision forced the victims' car off the road; it slammed into a tree and burst into flames. All the victims were badly injured. Both perpetrators were prosecuted under the new federal law.

Popejoy, who pleaded guilty, was sentenced to four years in prison. Maybee was convicted after a jury trial and received a prison term of eleven years. "The facts of this case shock the conscience," said assistant US attorney general Thomas E. Perez. "Five men were almost killed for no reason other than the fact that they are Hispanic. The Shepard-Byrd Hate Crimes Prevention Act allowed us to bring these men to justice in a way that we could not have done just a few years ago. These sentences send a clear message that the Justice Department will aggressively prosecute those who perpetrate violent acts of hate."[47]

> **"The Shepard-Byrd Hate Crimes Prevention Act allowed us to bring these men to justice in a way that we could not have done just a few years ago."[47]**
>
> —Assistant US attorney general Thomas E. Perez

Although states started passing their own hate crime laws during the 1980s, it took the deaths of two innocent victims, Shepard and Byrd, for a national dialogue to emerge, eventually leading to adoption of a tough, comprehensive federal law. Even with passage of the federal law, that dialogue continues.

The Challenges of Bringing Perpetrators to Justice

Shiraz Khan was driving home from work in the British city of Manchester in June 2017 when a car pulled alongside his vehicle. The two men in the car signaled him to pull over, shouting at him that his car had a flat tire. Khan slowed to a stop, got out of his car, and inspected his tires—but he did not see a flat. By now, the other car had stopped as well. Khan recalls, "While I was looking at it one of the guys said, 'We're only joking. You're a terrorist bomber.'"[48] The man then attempted to strike Khan across the face with a glass bottle.

Khan managed to block the blow with his hand, but he was still injured. His hand sustained deep wounds that had to be treated at a hospital. After the assault, the two men got back into their car and drove away. Khan decided not to tell police about the incident because he feared that if the news media covered the story, his photo would be published and that could lead to others targeting him for assault. He said, "I don't want anything to happen again. I don't want my picture going around anywhere and for me to become a target. . . . I'm just happy I've defended my face, and it's only my hand [that has] been injured."[49]

According to police in Manchester, Khan is not the first Muslim in their city to have been assaulted by perpetrators of hate crimes, nor is he the first Muslim to decline to report the incident to police. Wasim Chaudhry, the superintendent of police in Manchester, said many Muslims do not believe they will find protection from police; moreover, like Khan, many fear retribution if they report the attacks. Chaudhry insisted, though, that police in Manchester would vigorously pursue the perpetrators. He asserted, "If the perpetrators are left unchecked, and if their behaviour is not tackled, then [they will] undertake further victimisation that can increase in terms of its gravity."[50]

> "I don't want anything to happen again. I don't want my picture going around anywhere and for me to become a target. . . . I'm just happy I've defended my face, and it's only my hand [that has] been injured."[49]
>
> —Shiraz Khan, a hate crime victim in Manchester, Great Britain

Authorities in America have encountered a similar reluctance by hate crime victims to report the attacks against them. In 2017 the US Bureau of Justice Statistics, an agency of the federal government, released a report detailing the frequency of hate crimes committed in America from 2004 to 2015. One of the most startling facts uncovered by the report is that some 50 percent of hate crimes go unreported to police. According to the report, "About a quarter of hate crime victims who did not report the crime believed that police would not want to be bothered or to get involved, would be inefficient or ineffective, or would cause trouble for the victim. About one in five crime victims stated that the victimization was not important enough to report to police."[51]

Apathetic Police

In fact, many hate crime victims suspect police will be apathetic toward their plights. Phyllis B. Gerstenfeld, a California State University psychology professor, recalls a case in which one of her students was victimized by a hate crime: a vandal painted antigay slurs on the student's garage and front door. In this case, the student did report the incident to police. "Two officers soon arrived and made a report," Gerstenfeld relates.

> They were polite, but before they left, one of them turned to her and said, "You know, if you don't want this to happen, you shouldn't be so obvious about being a lesbian." Speaking to me about this incident some months later, my student was angry at the police. Not only did she believe that they had insulted her, but she also thought that they were blaming her for being a victim. She felt victimized twice: once by the vandal and then again by the police. "If that ever happens to me again," she told me, "I won't call the police."[52]

In 2017, a government report uncovered that some 50 percent of hate crimes go unreported to police. Experts believe that many hate crime victims feel the police are indifferent or even apathetic toward their plights.

In 2017 a gay African American man attending a political rally in Denver, Colorado, said a passenger in a passing vehicle threw an egg at him, striking him in the face. Numerous members of the Denver gay community were in attendance at the event. The victim says he called the Denver police to report the incident but found the dispatcher unsympathetic: "No police officer came to my assistance, although I felt I was in distress."[53] And in a nearby Denver suburb, a lesbian says she believes a neighbor purposely tried to hit her with his car. She says she called police, albeit reluctantly. "I often think I will not be believed or taken seriously,"[54] she explains.

Law enforcement officials insist, however, that their departments do enforce all laws, including the laws established to combat hate crimes. In Denver, police spokesperson Christine Downs states that her department urges all citizens to report crimes: "The Denver Police Department strongly encourages all residents to report crime, regardless of how insignificant they may think it is, especially bias-motivated crimes."[55] Moreover, in 2017 US attorney general Jeff Sessions, regarded as the nation's chief prosecutor, declared, "I have directed all of our federal prosecutors to make violent crime prosecution a top priority, and you can be sure this includes hate crimes. We will demand and expect results."[56]

"I have directed all of our federal prosecutors to make violent crime prosecution a top priority, and you can be sure this includes hate crimes. We will demand and expect results."[56]

—US attorney general Jeff Sessions

Inaccurate Statistics

The continuing hesitancy of many victims to report hate crimes to police may be a reason for a decrease in the number of incidents reported over the past decade. According to the FBI, the number of hate crimes reported in 2016—6,121 incidents—is significantly lower than the number of incidents reported in 2006. That year, 7,722 hate crime incidents were reported by police.

Many experts agree that bias has not eased in American society over the past decade. A 2018 study released by the Intelligence Project, a program sponsored by the SPLC, found that the number of hate groups in the United States has risen since 2015, when 892 such groups were in existence. In 2017 the SPLC said 954 hate groups were in existence in the United States. "This has been a year that has seen increasing divisiveness and bigotry, particularly in the mainstream of American life,"[57] insisted Heidi Beirich, director of the Intelligence Project.

Experts argue, then, that despite what the FBI may report, hate crimes have not decreased over the past several years but, rather, have been on the increase. They argue the FBI statistics do not reflect the true number of hate crimes committed in the United States. In fact, the Bureau of Justice Statistics study suggested that as many as 250,000 hate crimes are committed each year. The bureau arrived at that number through the annual National Crime Victimization Survey, which is sent out each year to some 135,000 households in the United States. People who respond to the survey are asked whether they were victims of crimes and, if they were, to describe the crimes. The agency then employs a statistical analysis to provide national averages for various offenses, including hate crimes. Therefore, the number of hate crimes reported by the Bureau of Justice Statistics is considerably greater than the number reported by the FBI because the survey seeks its information from victims whereas the FBI reports data reported to the agency by police departments.

The reluctance of victims to report the crimes may be a prime reason for the underreporting of hate crimes, but there may be other factors as well. For example, federal law defines a hate crime as a "criminal offense against a person or property motivated in whole or in part by an offender's bias against a race, religion, disability, sexual orientation, ethnicity, gender, or gender identity."[58] But that is not how many states define hate crimes. Prosecutors in Montana, for example, can apply their state's hate crime law to offenders who commit crimes perpetrated on the basis of bias only against race, ethnicity, or religion. It means disabled people as well as gay and transgender people are not protected under Montana's hate crime law. "If these crimes are never really counted, it's a way of saying they are not important,"[59] says Mark Potok, a spokesperson for the SPLC.

"If these crimes are never really counted, it's a way of saying they are not important."[59]

—Mark Potok, a spokesperson for the Southern Poverty Law Center

Wide Discrepancies

Laws in many other states are hardly comprehensive. For example, Idaho's law applies to religious bias as well as racial or ethnic bias, but it does not protect gay and transgender people. Maine's law protects people against bias based on religion, race, and ethnicity. Maine's law also protects gay people—but not transgender people—against crimes of bias.

Therefore, when police in Maine report crimes of bias to the FBI, they do not include crimes against transgender people. Crimes perpetrated by bias against gay and transgender people as well as disabled people also are left out of the statistics reported by North Dakota police to the FBI. Crimes against gay and

A young man suffering from cerebral palsy stands with assistance from his grandmother. Hate crime definitions vary widely from state to state. In many states, crimes against disabled people are not considered hate crimes.

transgender people are, likewise, left out of Idaho's report to the FBI. Kentucky police report crimes against gay people but not crimes against transgender people.

The wide discrepancy in what can be regarded as hate crimes in each state is a major factor in one statistic uncovered by ProPublica, a foundation based in New York City that pursues investigative journalism. In 2016 ProPublica found that nearly 90 percent of law enforcement agencies in America reported no hate crimes committed in their jurisdictions. In fact, the FBI reported similar findings in its 2016 statistics. According to the agency, it sought hate crime reports from 15,254 police departments in the United States and received responses from just 1,776, meaning just about 11 percent of police departments in America reported hate crimes in 2016. According to ProPublica, the low rate of hate crimes reported by local police can be attributed to a number of factors. Among them are lax reporting

Little Training for Police

One reason why many hate crimes go unreported is the lack of training for police officers, who simply may not know how to recognize a hate crime. A 2017 study by ProPublica determined that just nine states mandate that state and municipal police officers undergo training to recognize and respond to crimes of bias. "Police don't always get training on hate crimes," says Rachel Glickhouse, manager of the ProPublica hate crimes project. "They may not know how to identify one. So we've found a lot of confusion on the local level about how to identify hate crime and how to track a hate crime."

The police department of Seattle, Washington, provides a typical example. A 2017 study conducted by the Seattle Office of City Auditor found that cadets at the state's police academy receive some training on identifying and responding to hate crimes, but there is no follow-up education for police officers once they join the Seattle force. According to the report, "Seattle PD does not provide any hate crime training to its officers as a refresher or to build on the Academy training. Training is crucial for police officers to accurately identify a hate crime and respond appropriately." In contrast to Seattle, some major city police departments train detectives to investigate crimes of bias, assigning them to hate crimes task forces. Among the city police departments with such task forces are New York City, Philadelphia, and San Francisco.

Quoted in Alison Stewart, "Police Often Ill-Equipped to Handle Hate Crimes," *PBS NewsHour,* December 31, 2017. www.pbs.org.

Melissa Alderson and Claudia Gross-Shader, *Review of Hate Crime Prevention, Response, and Reporting in Seattle, Phase 1 Report*. Seattle Office of City Auditor, September 2017, p. 14. www.seattle.gov.

by police, inability of many police agencies to recognize hate crimes, and a tendency by many local police departments to simply ignore hate crime cases.

Few Federal Prosecutions

One of the purposes of the Shepard-Byrd act was to give the federal government authority to step in and pursue hate crime cases when local police and prosecutors decline to act. And with a large percentage of local police departments either failing to recognize hate crimes or outright ignoring the offenses it would seem as though the US Justice Department and FBI would be very busy investigating and prosecuting hate crime cases.

But that has not been the case. A 2015 Syracuse University study found that between 2009, when the Shepard-Byrd act law was adopted, and May 2015, the Justice Department was asked by local authorities to prosecute 270 hate crime cases. Of those 270 referrals, federal prosecutors turned down 235 cases. Of the thirty-five individuals prosecuted by the Justice Department, twenty-nine were convicted of hate crimes and six were found not guilty. The Syracuse University study found one major reason for the Justice Department's failure to pursue prosecutions in those 235 cases: Justice Department attorneys concluded that the cases lacked sufficient evidence to prove bias was a factor in the crime.

In fact, for federal prosecutors as well as local police and district attorneys who hope to pursue hate crime offenders, building solid cases of bias is not always automatic. The Syracuse study cited some typical findings:

> The Eastern District of Michigan (Detroit) leads the nation with the 19 federal hate crime referrals since the law's passage in 2009. However, of these only four were prosecuted, with just a single conviction resulting.
>
> The state of Idaho had the second largest number of federal hate crime referrals with 14. Two of these were prosecuted, but neither defendant was convicted.
>
> Tied for third place was the Northern District of California (San Francisco) and the state of Arizona, each with 12 federal hate crime referrals. Federal prosecutors in both districts turned down all of these without filing charges.[60]

Lacking Sufficient Evidence

The Syracuse study found that prosecutors in those jurisdictions found insufficient evidence to qualify the offenses as hate crimes. In the typical assault case, for example, a Hispanic or African

American or other member of a minority group may have heard racial or ethnic slurs uttered during the commission of a crime, but that does not mean the crime was motivated by bias.

Christopher Shaw, a senior prosecutor for the Weber County District Attorney's Office in Utah, points out that in a recent case he reviewed a Hispanic man and white man got into an altercation that turned into a fistfight. But just because the white man shouted anti-Hispanic slurs during the fight did not mean the brawl was instigated over bias. In Utah, Shaw notes, judges have ruled hate crimes must be motivated by the perpetrator's desire to deny a citizen's ability to exercise or enjoy his or her civil rights. "A bunch of white supremacists attacking some people of color—that's a hate crime," says Shaw. "In my view, you've got to have some evidence of a class of people specific to the conduct. There was a racial slur in an aggravated assault, a pretty ugly case, but from the evidence I can see, there was nothing that really jumped out at me as necessarily (carrying) a hate crime enhancement."[61]

"There was a racial slur in an aggravated assault, a pretty ugly case, but from the evidence I can see, there was nothing that really jumped out at me as necessarily (carrying) a hate crime enhancement."[61]

—Christopher Shaw, a senior prosecutor for the Weber County District Attorney's Office in Utah

Experts agree that proving the motivation behind the crime can be challenging. They contend that not only do prosecutors have to find evidence that the perpetrator is biased, but also that the bias was a driving factor in their decision to commit the crime. They point out that there is no law on the books anywhere in America that prohibits a person from harboring bias against a specific race, ethnic group, or sexual orientation—such personal prejudices do not qualify as hate crimes. As Jeannine Bell, a professor of law at Indiana University, explains, "It's not just that you dislike people of my background. You're entirely free to dislike people of my background. It's not that you tell me that you don't like me. Again, entirely free to do that. It's that you selected me for some sort of criminal action because of my background."[62]

Road Rage or Hate Crime?

In 2017 the question of whether Nabra Hassanen was victimized because of a bias harbored by her assailant was weighed by prosecutors in Virginia. Hassanen, a seventeen-year-old Muslim, was raped and murdered, allegedly by Darwin Torres. According to police, while Hassanen and some friends were riding their bicycles to a mosque in the city of Fairfax, they got into an altercation with Torres. Police said twenty-two-year-old Torres pursued the girls in his car, caught up with Hassanen, and struck her with a baseball bat. He allegedly sexually assaulted the victim before striking her again, killing her, and then dumping her body in a pond.

The victim's father, Mohmoud Hassanen, insisted that Torres should be charged with a hate crime. "He followed the girls, and all of them had head cloths, meaning they are Muslim, and he had a baseball stick. He was running behind these kids. I told the detective: 'I want to ask him one question. Why did he do that? Because he doesn't like Muslims, or what?' He tells me he has no answer for that."[63]

Attendees mourn at a vigil for Nabra Hassanen, a teenage Muslim girl killed by a man near a mosque in Virginia. Whether the case is a hate crime is debated.

Hate Crimes and Clerical Errors

A probe by ProPublica found a major reason why many hate crime cases go unreported to the FBI: clerical errors.

The organization reviewed hate crime incident reports from several police departments and found that police officers had, in fact, properly responded to the incidents and filed reports on their investigations, but those reports were not included in statistics that were eventually reported to the FBI. The FBI issues annual statistics on the number and nature of hate crime incidents in the United States. ProPublica concluded that some police departments are guilty of sloppy record keeping, citing two examples in a December 2017 study on how police departments report hate crimes:

> The Miami-Dade Police Department started an internal audit after we talked to them in October. Detective Carlos Rosario, a spokesman for the department, told us they found four hate crimes that they had failed to report to the state. Rosario also told us that they are in the process of creating a digital hate crime reporting process as a result of our reporting.
>
> The Colorado Springs, Colorado, police department fixed a database problem that had caused the loss of at least 18 hate crime reports. The error was discovered after we asked them questions about their records.

Rachel Glickhouse, "What We Discovered During a Year of Documenting Hate," ProPublica, December 26, 2017. www.propublica.org.

Under Virginia law, Torres could have been charged with a hate crime if prosecutors were prepared to allege that the crime was motivated by a bias against a religious faith or ethnic group. But, ultimately, Torres was not charged with a hate crime. Prosecutors concluded that what led to the crime was more akin to a road rage incident. "There is nothing at this point to indicate that this tragic case was a hate crime,"[64] commented Julie Parker, a spokesperson for the Fairfax Police Department.

Torres was charged with the rape and murder of Hassanen. Although he was not charged with a hate crime, if convicted, it is likely he will face the harshest penalty available under Virginia law. Prosecutors have announced they plan to pursue the death penalty against Torres.

Prosecutors face many hurdles if they expect to bring successful hate crime cases against perpetrators. Those hurdles may often include the police officers investigating the cases—many victims believe police display apathetic attitudes toward them. Meanwhile, the definition of what qualifies as a hate crime varies widely from state to state, meaning many victims are not receiving the protections under laws intended to safeguard them from perpetrators who single them out for attack.

What Can Be Done About Hate Crimes?

Joe Bednarksy Jr. joined the Ku Klux Klan at the age of eighteen. For years, Bednarsky was a dedicated Klansmen—he traveled the country attending rallies and handing out racist pamphlets at farm shows and other public events. He wore the white robes of the group and had the letters *KKK* tattooed onto his hand. Soon, Bednarsky rose to a leadership position in a Klan chapter near his home in Millville, New Jersey.

In 1996 Bednarsky shot an African American woman with a slingshot, striking her in the leg. He was arrested and convicted under New Jersey's hate crime law; he spent a year in prison. After leaving prison, Bednarsky at first returned to the Klan, but over the next few years he found himself questioning the values that had dominated most of his life. Finally, in 2007, Bednarsky saw the injustice in the culture of which he had been a part. He knew he had to change his life. "I was either going to end up dead somewhere or end up in prison for the rest of my life,"[65] he says. He quit the Klan and burned his robes.

A short time later, Bednarsky started attending services at Bethel African Methodist Episcopal Church in Millville, which has an all–African American congregation. Congregants were at first suspicious of Bednarsky—they knew he had been a Klansman. The church's minister, the Reverend Charles E. Wilkins, warily approached Bednarsky to find out why he had started coming to the church. Wilkins says, "We started talking, and I think the first time I really took note and realized something was different was when he said, 'Brother, where there's God's grace there is no race. And I'm thinking, 'OK, that sounds good.' He told me God changed his heart and if I don't believe that, I need to get another job. I had to take him for his word."[66]

Wilkins and the congregants of his church decided to accept Bednarsky. In fact, Wilkins gave Bednarsky a job: he appointed him security director for the church. Bednarsky stands 6 feet 6 inches (198 cm) tall and weighs 330 pounds (150 kg). He holds a black belt in the martial art tae kwon do. If anybody intends to commit a hate crime at Bethel African Methodist Episcopal Church, they have to go through Bednarsky first.

Capable of Rehabilitation

Bednarsky's change of heart illustrates that people who have committed hate crimes are capable of rehabilitation. Christian Picciolini of Chicago, Illinois, underwent a similar conversion. At the age of fourteen he joined a neo-Nazi group known as the Hammerskin Nation. Members of the group sought out African Americans, gays, Jews, and others, targeting them for violent acts. "I felt a sort of energy flow through me that I had never felt before," Picciolini said of his eight years in the Hammerskin Nation, "as if I was a part of something greater than myself."[67]

Some people who have committed hate crimes are capable of rehabilitation. Sometimes simple interaction with those they once harbored resentment toward can change the hateful feelings these perpetrators once had.

But in 2011, while assaulting an African American man, Picciolini said he suddenly realized what he was doing was wrong. Picciolini locked eyes with the victim, and immediately felt a strong sense of empathy for the man. Picciolini withdrew from the assault. Over the next five years he wrestled with his conscience. He fell into a deep depression. His wife left him, taking the couple's child with her. Finally, he decided to turn his life around. Picciolini quit the Hammerskins and opened his mind to the people around him. He befriended African Americans, Jews, and others, and he found them to be kind and caring individuals who refused to hate others. "I had never in my life engaged in a meaningful dialogue with the people that I thought I hated, and it was these folks who showed me empathy when I least deserved it, and they were the ones that I least deserved it from," he says.

"I had never in my life engaged in a meaningful dialogue with the people that I thought I hated, and it was these folks who showed me empathy when I least deserved it, and they were the ones that I least deserved it from."[68]

—Christian Picciolini, a former neo-Nazi

> I started to recognize that I had more in common with them than the people I had surrounded myself for eight years with—that these people, that I thought I hated, took it upon themselves to see something inside of me that I didn't even see myself, and it was because of that connection that I was able to humanize them and that destroyed the demonization and the prejudice that was happening inside of me.[68]

Eventually, Picciolini founded Life After Hate. The group is devoted to convincing members of hate groups to leave their organizations, learn about equality and inclusion, and start new lives.

Bias Incidents Are Increasing

Although it is possible for people who have committed hate crimes to learn to lose their prejudices, cases like those of Bednarsky and Picciolini are not all that common. In fact, organizations that track

Indian Americans Mobilize Against Hate

The 2017 murder of Srinivas Kuchibhotla in Olathe, Kansas, alerted many Indian Americans to a sad truth: They, too, could be victims of hate crimes. Prior to his murder, many immigrants from India had settled into comfortable lives and believed they were immune from hate crimes. Following the murder of Kuchibhotla, several Indian American business leaders and others banded together to form the Indian American Impact Project. The goal of the organization is to elect Indian Americans to political office so they can help write laws that encourage equality and inclusion while fighting hate crimes.

"They thought they were safe," says California activist Anirvan Chatterjee. "They thought their bindis would protect them, they thought their last names would protect them, they thought their advanced degrees would protect them, and something changed." (A bindi is a decorative mark often worn by Indian women on their foreheads.)

In 2018, the Impact Project supported eight candidates for Congress and state legislative seats. According to a statement by the Impact Project,

> Despite rapid growth and professional success, for too long Indian Americans have been underrepresented in elected office from state capitols to the US Congress. As a result, our needs, concerns, and priorities often go unheard in the halls of power. At a time when our community and our values are under attack by [racist] rhetoric and regressive policies, it is more critical than ever that Indian Americans build and wield political power to fight back.

Quoted in Arun Venugopal, "Indian Americans Reckon with Reality of Hate Crimes," *Code Switch*, NPR, May 15, 2017. www.npr.org.

Indian American Impact Project, "About Impact," 2018. https://iaimpact.org.

hate crimes say that reports of bias incidents are increasing. In one study, the Anti-Defamation League (ADL) reported the number of anti-Semitic incidents at 1,266 in 2016, an increase of 34 percent over the previous year. Such incidents range from the bullying of Jewish children to acts of vandalism at synagogues. Moreover, 2017 saw an even greater increase—the ADL reported 1,986 incidents that year, a hike of 60 percent over the previous year.

Other groups have also seen a hike in hate crime. From 2008 through 2014, the Los Angeles Commission on Human Relations reported a drop in hate crimes targeting Hispanic Americans, but 2015 saw a sudden increase in such offenses. That year, the agency noted that sixty-one hate crimes were committed against Hispanic Americans in the city, compared to thirty-four the year before. In 2016, the commission reported, sixty-two hate crimes were committed against Hispanic Americans. "We are extremely concerned that reported hate crimes increased dramatically in 2015," says Robin Toma, the executive director of the commission. "The disturbing rise in bias-motivated crime indicates that, despite the gains made by historically marginalized communities, bigoted attacks are still a daily occurrence, and that is unacceptable."[69]

Changing Young Minds

Some groups are trying to change this mindset. They have created programs for students in kindergarten through college; these programs are intended to build respect, tolerance, and empathy. One such program, called Not in Our School, was developed by a group based in Oakland, California, called Not in Our Town (NIOT). The group's goal is to teach elementary, middle, and high school students about equality and inclusion—and, in the process, to create safe school environments for all students.

Teachers who participate in the Not in Our School program incorporate antihate themes into their lesson plans. For example, in 2011 teachers at Gunn High School in Palo Alto, California, devoted a full week to this subject in their classrooms. One teacher showed a video to the class from the NIOT series *What Would You Do?* The video featured two Hispanic American customers facing prejudice in a store, where a cashier refused to serve them. The video challenged students to speak up and defend the customers. The teacher comments, "I showed my [literature] class one of the *What Would You Do?* videos . . . to very good effect. One student said, 'I think it's great we are learning about these things in this school. At my old school, which was in a violent and dangerous area, we never learned anything about this.'"[70]

Meanwhile, another teacher led a discussion on discrimination. According to the teacher,

> [There was] interesting feedback from the students that Gunn is diverse yet students are still unfairly judged. Then, I had them think of an experience where they felt unfairly judged or discriminated against or so forth. . . . It went really well and the kids were responsive. I did have some students who had experiences that we could all learn from and I did have one student that I had to talk to outside of the classroom during the activity because it really hit home.[71]

Another program that works to eliminate hate was established in 2018 by the ADL. The program is aimed at educating college students about the dangers of hate speech and hate crimes. Known as Innovate Against Hate, the project provides $1,000 grants to individual students or groups of students on twenty college campuses. (The ADL hopes to expand the program to all college campuses.) The students are challenged to develop innovative programs helping others understand the importance of equality and tolerance. "One of the biggest challenges facing campus communities is the prevalence of hate speech and hate group activity on campus," says George Selim, vice president of programs for ADL. "Students are well-versed in social media and have credibility with their peers. They can play a pivotal role in fighting against hate and extremism, and arming them with the tools to do so now will build a generation of change-makers."[72]

> **"Students are well-versed in social media and have credibility with their peers. They can play a pivotal role in fighting against hate and extremism."[72]**
>
> —George Selim, the vice president of programs at the Anti-Defamation League

The Need for New Hate Crime Laws

Civil rights groups also hope to address hate crimes by getting lawmakers to take a fresh look at state and national hate crime laws. The ADL, for example, hopes to convince lawmakers in the five states lacking such laws to finally place hate crime laws on their books. The ADL initiated its campaign, which it named 50 States Against Hate, in 2015, shortly after the nine murders committed by Dylann Roof in Charleston. "The recent hate-based murders in Charleston by a white supremacist is a wake-up call that the time is now to bring strong hate crime laws to all fifty states," ADL national director Jonathan A. Greenblatt said at the time.

However, by 2018—three years after the ADL initiated the program—none of the states lacking hate crime laws had adopted such laws. Moreover, efforts to strengthen hate crime laws on the federal level have also fallen short. In 2017 Representatives Barbara Comstock of Virginia and Debbie Dingell of Michigan introduced a measure in the House of Representatives to update reporting requirements for hate crimes. The bill attempted to standardize the definitions of hate crimes from state

Congresswoman Debbie Dingell speaks at an event in Michigan in 2017. Dingell, along with representative Barbara Comstock, has introduced a measure in Congress to update hate crime reporting.

to state, enabling the FBI to gather more accurate information on hate crime trends. The measure would also create a task force composed of representatives from several federal agencies to develop a national strategy to combat hate crimes. As of mid-2018, the measure had failed to garner enough support to come up for a vote in Congress.

A Divisive Presidential Campaign

As officials at the ADL as well as the Los Angeles Commission on Human Relations observed, hate crimes as well as hate-inspired rhetoric ramped up significantly in 2015 and 2016. Many experts point to the divisive 2016 presidential campaign in which Republican nominee Donald Trump, the eventual winner, often spiced his campaign with anti-immigrant rhetoric. When Trump opened his campaign in 2015, he had this to say about immigrants from Mexico: "When Mexico sends its people, they're not sending their best. They're not sending you. . . . They're sending people that have lots of problems, and they're bringing those problems with us. They're bringing drugs. They're bringing crime. They're rapists. And some, I assume, are good people."[73]

Moreover, during the campaign Trump promised to enact a travel ban on immigrants from several Middle Eastern nations, all with populations composed mainly of Muslims. In a nationally televised interview, Trump defended the ban by saying, "I think Islam hates us."[74] Trump has said he believes the travel ban is necessary to reduce the threat of Islamist-inspired terrorism against Americans.

After winning the election, Trump ordered the ban, which was challenged in federal court but went into effect in 2017. Further court challenges were pending in 2018. After those court challenges are heard, the US Supreme Court is expected to make a final decision on the legality of the ban, which critics suggest is aimed at blocking Muslims from entering the country and, therefore, violates their constitutional right to freedom of religion.

Hearing such rhetoric from a political leader emboldened many people to become more public with their prejudices. Many have brazenly marched in the streets, denouncing immigrants

New Protections for Transgender People in Canada

Lawmakers in Canada adopted a new law in 2017 providing transgender people with protections under the country's hate crime laws. (Transgender people had been left out of previous hate crime protections in Canada.) Specifically, the law provides harsh sentencing provisions. If a Canadian court finds that a perpetrator targeted a person specifically because of the victim's gender identity, the court could regard the perpetrator's bias as an aggravating factor and make the sentence harsher. "This bill is not only about the protections it provides, but also the message that Parliament is delivering to all Canadians about the need to treat everybody equally," says Senator Grant Mitchell, who represents the province of Alberta in the Canadian parliament. "Transgender and gender-diverse people deserve to know that they are welcome and accepted, embraced and protected, and that in Canada they are free to be their true selves."

Quoted in John Paul Trasker, "Canada Enacts Protections for Transgender Community," CBC News, June 16, 2017. www.cbc.ca.

and members of minority groups. As the statistics gathered by the ADL and the Los Angeles Commission on Human Relations suggest, others resorted to committing hate crimes. In fact, in the month following the November 2016 presidential election, the SPLC cataloged 1,094 bias-related incidents.

On August 12, 2017, emotions reached a boiling point when groups of white supremacists descended on Charlottesville, Virginia, for what they called the Unite the Right Rally. The purpose of the rally was to protest the removal of a statue honoring Confederate army general Robert E. Lee from a public square in Charlottesville. White supremacist leaders also hoped to use the event to unify their followers in a campaign to call for the separation of the races in American society. Among their demands are the outlawing of interracial marriage as well as prohibitions against immigration of nonwhites into the United States.

As members of the KKK and neo-Nazi groups marched, counterprotesters staged their own rally nearby. Suddenly, a car driven by an avowed white supremacist, James Alex Fields Jr., drove into a group of counterprotesters, killing one woman, thirty-two-year-old Heather Heyer, and injuring thirty-five others. Fields was charged with murdering Heyer, and faces possible life imprisonment.

Prosecutors considered charging Fields with a hate crime but decided they might not be able to prove their case. They concluded that Heyer, a white woman, would not ordinarily be targeted by a white supremacist and therefore a hate crime charge might not fit under either Virginia law or the federal statute. "The dead person in this case doesn't necessarily meet the animosity of the

In 2017, white nationalist groups with torches marched through the streets of Charlottesville, Virginia, in the Unite the Right Rally. Counterprotests led to a confrontation that resulted in the death of a woman and injuries to thirty-five others.

alleged perpetrator," said Horace Cooper, a former constitutional law professor at George Mason University in Virginia. He added that a defense attorney could contend, "Was it racial supremacy views or was it road rage?"[75]

Achieving More Political Power

With new hate crime laws in state legislatures as well as Congress stalled, and with emotions over the president's views on immigration leading to such incidents as the Charlottesville rally, many civil rights activists believe the only way to tamp down hate is for people who believe in equality and inclusion to achieve more political power. In 2017 and 2018 the ranks of candidates for local and state offices as well as seats in Congress swelled with African Americans, Hispanic Americans, Asian Americans, and members from other minority groups. Many gay candidates stepped up to seek elective office. In Virginia, the site of the Charlottesville rally, two Hispanic American candidates, two Asian American candidates, and a transgender woman entered races for seats in the state legislature. In Durham, North Carolina, Vernetta Alston, a gay African American woman, won a seat on the city council in 2017. In Illinois, Lauren Underwood, an African American woman, announced her candidacy in 2018 for Congress. "I feel like every day there's a battle for the core of our democracy," she says. "People are stepping up and doing things they've never done before."[76]

And in Texas, Gina Ortiz Jones, a gay woman from San Antonio, also announced her candidacy for Congress. "I would be honored to be the first 'out' member of Congress for Texas," she said, "but it's more important that I'm not the last."[77] (The term *out* refers to a person who has publicly acknowledged he or she is gay.)

In 2017 Wilmot Collins was elected the first African American mayor of Helena, Montana. He arrived in Helena in 1990. Collins and his wife, Maddie, were refugees from Liberia, a war-torn and impoverished nation in Africa. Soon after finding a home in Helena, Collins awoke one morning to find someone had painted the words *KKK* and *Go back to Africa* on the wall of his garage. Collins called the police and then went back outside to discover that his neighbors had gathered together and were scrubbing the hateful words off his garage wall.

> **"You've seen racist stuff all over the country. But the reaction to mine was unique. And that says a lot about my community."[78]**
>
> **—Mayor Wilmot Collins of Helena, Montana**

Collins said the reaction by his neighbors touched him deeply. Their deeds gave Collins a feeling of strength, proving to him that he had made the right decision to immigrate to America. The sense of community they showed also proved to Collins that Helena is composed of people who accept newcomers and that people who commit hate crimes are members of a small minority. "You've seen racist stuff all over the country," he says. "But the reaction to mine was unique. And that says a lot about my community. That says a lot about where I live. That says a lot about the people of this Helena community."[78]

Whether the elections of these candidates and others eventually result in the drafting of new hate crime laws remains to be seen. Clearly, though, these candidates and others are committed to establishing a new national dialogue on hate that they hope will lead not only to new and tougher laws but also to a new culture of equality and inclusion for all.

SOURCE NOTES

Introduction: A Callous Hatred

1. Quoted in Jenny Jarvie, "Dylann Roof Trial: 'He Put Five Bullets in My Son,' Church Attack Survivor Testifies," *Los Angeles Times*, December 7, 2016. www.latimes.com.
2. Carolyn Turpin-Petrosino, *Understanding Hate Crimes: Acts, Motives, Offenders, Victims, and Justice*. New York: Routledge, 2015, p. 24.
3. Quoted in Allison Brophy Champion, "Orange Police Investigating Racist Vandalism as Hate Crime," *Culpeper Star-Exponent* (Culpeper County, VA), February 26, 2018. www.fredericksburg.com.
4. Quoted in Champion, "Orange Police Investigating Racist Vandalism as Hate Crime."
5. Quoted in Gretel Kauffman, "What Motivated Dylann Roof? Confession Offers Clues," *Christian Science Monitor*, December 11, 2016. www.csmonitor.com.

Chapter One: How Serious a Problem Are Hate Crimes?

6. Nancy Turner, "Responding to Hate Crimes: A Police Officer's Guide to Investigation and Prevention," in *Hate Crimes: A Reference Handbook*, ed. Donald Altschiller. Santa Barbara, CA: ABC-CLIO, 2005, pp. 111–12.
7. Quoted in Michael P. Rellahan, "Man Gets 3–6 Years in Jail for Sucker-Punching Disabled Man," *Delaware County (PA) Times*, November 29, 2017. www.delcotimes.com.
8. Phyllis B. Gerstenfeld, *Hate Crimes: Causes, Controls, and Controversies*. Los Angeles: Sage, 2018, p. 99.
9. Gerstenfeld, *Hate Crimes*, pp. 106–7.
10. Southern Poverty Law Center, "Ten Ways to Fight Hate: A Community Response Guide," August 14, 2017. www.splcenter.org.
11. Quoted in Breanna Edwards, "Man's Oregon Home Vandalized with Racist, Threatening Messages," *Root*, March 30, 2017. www.theroot.com.
12. Quoted in Edwards, "Man's Oregon Home Vandalized with Racist, Threatening Messages."

13. Quoted in Edwards, "Man's Oregon Home Vandalized with Racist, Threatening Messages."
14. Gerstenfeld, *Hate Crimes*, p. 99.
15. Gerstenfeld, *Hate Crimes*, p. 200.
16. Gerstenfeld, *Hate Crimes*, p. 209.
17. Quoted in Bob Brooks, "Hundreds of Headstones Vandalized at Philadelphia Jewish Cemetery," 6ABC Action News, February 27, 2017. http://6abc.com.
18. Turpin-Petrosino, *Understanding Hate Crimes*, p. 157.

Chapter Two: How Are People Hurt by Hate Crimes?

19. Quoted in WPXI News, "'I Feel Rage': Friends of Gay Man Attacked in Lawrenceville Demand Justice," October 7, 2013. www.wpxi.com.
20. Quoted in Matt Belanger and Bob Mayo, "Rally Shows Support for Gay Man Assaulted in Lawrenceville," Pittsburgh's Action News 4, October 7, 2013. www.wtae.com.
21. Erin M. Sanders-Haas, *The Impact of Hate Crime Trauma on Gay and Lesbian Interpersonal Relationships*. Manhattan: Kansas State University, 2008, p. 14. http://krex.k-state.edu.
22. Quoted in Sanders-Haas, *The Impact of Hate Crime Trauma on Gay and Lesbian Interpersonal Relationships*, p. 14.
23. Sanders-Haas, *The Impact of Hate Crime Trauma on Gay and Lesbian Interpersonal Relationships*, p. 14.
24. Quoted in Erika Pesantes, "Stabbed for Being Black—a Hate Crime Victim Recalls Not Wanting to Die," *Orlando Sun-Sentinel*, December 31, 2017. www.sun-sentinel.com.
25. Quoted in Pesantes, "Stabbed for Being Black."
26. Quoted in Christina Carrega-Woodby, "Brooklyn Creep Gets 20 Years for Brutal Plexiglass Attack on Transgender Woman," *New York Daily News*, January 14, 2016. www.nydailynews.com.
27. Quoted in Thomas Zambito, "Queens Man Daniel Aleman Sentenced to 8 Years in Gay-Bashing Attack," *New York Daily News*, December 14, 2010. www.nydailynews.com.
28. Quoted in Thomas Zambito, "Queens Gay Basher Daniel Rodriguez Gets 12 Years in Prison for Attack Outside Deli," *New York Daily News*, January 21, 2011. www.nydailynews.com.
29. Quoted in Audra D.S. Burch, "He Became a Hate Crime Victim. She Became a Widow," *New York Times*, July 8, 2017. www.nytimes.com.

30. Quoted in Yashwant Raj and Srinivasa Rao Apparasu, "Hyderabad Engineer Srinivas Kuchibhotla Shot Dead in US: What We Know So Far," *Hindustan Times*, March 15, 2017. www.hindustantimes.com.
31. Quoted in Burch, "He Became a Hate Crime Victim."
32. Quoted in Burch, "He Became a Hate Crime Victim."
33. Quoted in Heather Richards, "A Family Reflects Impact of Bullying, Depression on Gillette Man's Life," *Billings (MT) Gazette*, March 28, 2016. http://billingsgazette.com.
34. Quoted in Richards, "A Family Reflects Impact of Bullying, Depression on Gillette Man's Life."

Chapter Three: How Do Laws Address Hate Crimes?

35. Quoted in Antonia Blumberg, "Attackers Sentenced to 3 Years in Prison for Hate Crime Against Sikh Man," *Huffington Post*, May 19, 2017. www.huffingtonpost.com.
36. Quoted in Blumberg, "Attackers Sentenced to 3 Years in Prison for Hate Crime Against Sikh Man."
37. Quoted in Jo Josephson, "Hate and Bias: Maine's Attorney General and a Few Municipalities Have Responded to the Rise in Hate Crimes and Bias Incidents with Initiatives and Procedures," *Maine Townsman*, December 1993. www.memun.org.
38. Quoted in Tony Cook, "Indiana Lawmakers Take Up Hate Crimes Bill in Aftermath of Charlottesville," *Indianapolis Star*, January 22, 2018. www.indystar.com.
39. Quoted in WANE, "Push for Hate Crimes Law Fails Again in Indiana Legislature," January 30, 2018. www.wane.com.
40. Quoted in Aaron Schrank, "Riverton Detox Center Shooter Sentenced," Wyoming Public Media, January 11, 2016. http://wyomingpublicmedia.org.
41. Quoted in Laura Hancock, "Mead Says Wyoming Doesn't Need Hate Crimes Law," *Casper (WY) Star Tribune*, August 19, 2015. http://trib.com.
42. Quoted in Schrank, "Riverton Detox Center Shooter Sentenced."
43. Meredith Worden, "Justice for Hate Crimes: Commemorating the Signing of the Shepard/Byrd Act," Biography.com, October 28, 2015. www.biography.com.
44. Quoted in ABC News, "New Details Emerge in Matthew Shepard Murder," November 26, 2004. http://abcnews.go.com.
45. Turpin-Petrosino, *Understanding Hate Crimes*, p. 10.

46. Quoted in Martin Mbugua, "Hate Crimes Bill Drive Is On, Floral Park Rally Sparks Messages to State Senate," *New York Daily News*, November 21, 1999. www.nydailynews.com.
47. Quoted in US Justice Department, "Arkansas Men Sentenced for Federal Hate Crimes Related to the Assault of Five Hispanic Men," September 28, 2011. www.justice.gov.

Chapter Four: The Challenges of Bringing Perpetrators to Justice

48. Quoted in BBC News, "Manchester Attack: Fear 'Stops Muslims Reporting Hate Crime,'" June 6, 2017. www.bbc.com.
49. Quoted in BBC News, "Manchester Attack."
50. Quoted in BBC News, "Manchester Attack."
51. US Bureau of Justice Statistics, *Hate Crime Victimization, 2004–2015*, June 2017, p. 5. www.bjs.gov.
52. Gerstenfeld, *Hate Crimes*, p. 72.
53. Quoted in Ken Schwencke, "Confusion, Fear, Cynicism: Why People Don't Report Hate Incidents," ProPublica, July 31, 2017. www.propublica.org.
54. Quoted in Schwencke, "Confusion, Fear, Cynicism."
55. Quoted in Schwencke, "Confusion, Fear, Cynicism."
56. Quoted in Joe Sexton, "Victims in Thousands of Potential Hate Crimes Never Notify Police," ProPublica, June 29, 2017. www.propublica.org.
57. Quoted in Joe Heim, "Hate Groups in the US Remain on the Rise, According to New Study," *Washington Post*, February 21, 2018. www.washingtonpost.com.
58. Quoted in Mark Shenefelt, "2016 FBI Hate Crime Report Inaccurate for Northern Utah; Clerical Errors to Blame," *Ogden (UT) Standard-Examiner*, December 27, 2017. www.standard.net.
59. Quoted in *Chicago Tribune*, "Patchy Reporting Undercuts National Hate Crimes Count: AP Report," June 4, 2016. www.chicagotribune.com.
60. Syracuse University, *Convictions in Federal Hate Crime Cases Since FY 2010*, June 25, 2015. http://trac.syr.edu.
61. Quoted in Shenefelt, "2016 FBI Hate Crime Report Inaccurate for Northern Utah."
62. Quoted in German Lopez, "Why It's So Hard to Prosecute a Hate Crime," *Vox*, May 23, 2017. www.vox.com.
63. Quoted in Harriet Sinclair, "Who Is Darwin Martinez-Torres? Suspect in Murder of Muslim Teen Is Held by ICE," *Newsweek*, June 20, 2017. www.newsweek.com.

64. Quoted in Dakin Andone, David Shortell, and Darran Simon, "Police: Death of Muslim Girl Not Believed to Be Hate Crime," CNN, June 20, 2017. www.cnn.com.

Chapter Five: What Can Be Done About Hate Crimes?

65. Quoted in Jason Nark, "Atonement: Ex-Klan Leader Now Leads Security at Black Church," *Philadelphia Inquirer*, February 11, 2018, p. B3.
66. Quoted in Nark, "Atonement."
67. Quoted in Dave Davies, "A Former Neo-Nazi Explains Why Hate Drew Him In—and How He Got Out," NPR, January 18, 2018. www.npr.org.
68. Quoted in Davies, "A Former Neo-Nazi Explains Why Hate Drew Him In."
69. Quoted in Dennis Romero, "In the Era of Trump, Anti-Latino Hate Crimes Jumped 69% in LA," *LA Weekly*, September 29, 2016. www.laweekly.com.
70. Quoted in *Not in Our Town Blog*, "Teachers Share Lessons from Not in Our School Week," May 25, 2011. www.niot.org.
71. Quoted in *Not in Our Town Blog*, "Teachers Share Lessons from Not in Our School Week."
72. Quoted in Anti-Defamation League, "ADL Launches Student-Led Program to 'Innovate Against Hate,'" March 5, 2018. www.adl.org.
73. Quoted in Michelle Ye Hee Lee, "Donald Trump's False Comments Connecting Mexican Immigrants and Crime," *Washington Post*, July 8, 2015. www.washingtonpost.com.
74. Quoted in Theodore Schleifer, "Donald Trump: 'I Think Islam Hates Us,'" CNN, March 10, 2016. www.cnn.com.
75. Quoted in Fred Lucas, "Should Charlottesville Suspect Fields Be Charged with Terrorism or a Hate Crime?," *Newsweek*, August 15, 2017. www.newsweek.com.
76. Quoted in Juana Summers, "Candidates of Color Get Off the Sidelines in the Age of Trump," CNN, January 27, 2018. www.cnn.com.
77. Quoted in Julie Moreau, "Growing Number of LGBTQ Candidates Seek Political Office in 2018," NBC News, January 29, 2018. www.nbcnews.com.
78. Quoted in Lulu Garcia-Navarro, "Meet the Next Mayor of Helena, Montana," NPR, November 12, 2017. www.npr.org.

Anti-Defamation League (ADL)
605 Third Ave.
New York, NY 10158
www.adl.org

The ADL has pursued a number of programs to fight hate crimes, most significantly crafting model hate crime legislation and lobbying state legislators to pass antihate measures. By following the link for "What We Do" on the ADL website, visitors can find a number of resources on hate crimes, including the group's list of American cities that do not report hate crimes.

Canadian Department of Justice
284 Wellington St.
Ottawa, ON
Canada K1A 0H8
www.justice.gc.ca

Canada's Department of Justice oversees national law enforcement efforts in the country, including the prosecution of hate crimes. The department's website includes a page devoted to hate crimes titled "Disproportionate Harm: Hate Crime in Canada." The page includes a list of major police departments in Canada and how each defines crimes of bias.

European Union Agency for Fundamental Rights
Schwarzenbergplatz 11
A-1040 Vienna
Austria
http://fra.europa.eu/en

The agency studies human rights issues in Europe, including the prevalence of hate crimes. By accessing the link for "Hate Crimes" on the agency's website, visitors can find numerous reports, including studies of anti-Semitism in Europe, hate crimes against immigrants, and offenses committed against disabled children.

Federal Bureau of Investigation (FBI)
935 Pennsylvania Ave. NW
Washington, DC 20535
www.fbi.gov

The US government's chief law enforcement agency is responsible for enforcing federal hate crime laws. By entering the term *hate crimes* into the FBI website search engine, visitors can find a number of resources on hate crimes, including the FBI's year-by-year statistics on the number of hate crimes, as well as the nature of those crimes, that are committed in the United States.

Life After Hate
917 W. Washington Blvd., Suite 212
Chicago, IL 60607
www.lifeafterhate.org

This organization, founded by former neo-Nazi Christian Picciolini, helps members of hate groups start new lives, aiding them in learning about equality and inclusion. The group's programs include #WeCounterHate, which searches for hate speech on Twitter, then counters those Twitter feeds with positive messages.

Matthew Shepard Foundation
800 Eighteenth St., Suite 101
Denver, CO 80202
www.matthewshepard.org

Founded after the death of Matthew Shepard, the foundation pursues a number of projects to combat hate crimes. By following the link for "Hate Crimes Work" on the organization's website, visitors can find charts and graphs showing the prevalence of hate crimes in America. One map shows, state by state, the percentage of police agencies that report hate crimes to the FBI.

National Association for the Advancement of Colored People (NAACP)
4805 Mt. Hope Dr.
Baltimore, MD 21215
www.naacp.org

The NAACP has compiled a long record of fighting for the civil rights of African Americans. Among the organization's projects is the No Hate campaign, which works to persuade Congress to enact a tough antihate crime measure titled the National Opposition to Hate, Assault and Threats to Equality Act, abbreviated as the NO HATE Act. The measure was first introduced in Congress in 2017.

National LGBTQ Task Force

1325 Massachusetts Ave. NW, Suite 600
Washington, DC 20005
www.thetaskforce.org

The task force lobbies for the rights of gay and transgender citizens. By entering the term *hate crimes* in the search engine on the task force website, visitors can find many updates on hate crime issues, including a map showing how each state's hate crime laws address protections for gay and transgender people.

Not in Our Town (NIOT)

PO Box 70232
Oakland, CA 94612
www.niot.org

Not in Our Town oversees a number of projects to combat hate crimes, including workshops for city and town leaders as well as teachers and school administrators on how to recognize and react to hate crimes, hate speech, and bullying. Visitors to the organization's website can view the PBS documentary on the group, *Not in Our Town: Billings, Montana*.

Southern Poverty Law Center (SPLC)

400 Washington Ave.
Montgomery, AL 36104
www.splcenter.org

The SPLC monitors hate groups in America, reporting on their activities and rhetoric. The organization has made a number of its reports available on its website, including *Extremist Files*, which lists the most prominent hate groups in the United States, and a hate map, which shows city-by-city locations of more than nine hundred American hate groups.

Books

Edward Dunbar, *Hate Unleashed: America's Cataclysmic Change*. Santa Barbara, CA: Praeger, 2017.

Phyllis B. Gerstenfeld, *Hate Crimes: Causes, Controls, and Controversies*. Los Angeles: Sage, 2018.

Ibram X. Kendi, *Stamped from the Beginning: The Definitive History of Racist Ideas in America*. New York: Nation, 2017.

Christian Picciolini, *White American Youth: My Descent into America's Most Violent Hate Movement—and How I Got Out*. New York: Hachette, 2017.

Carolyn Turpin-Petrosino, *Understanding Hate Crimes: Acts, Motives, Offenders, Victims, and Justice*. New York: Routledge, 2015.

Internet Sources

Audra D.S. Burch, "He Became a Hate Crime Victim. She Became a Widow," *New York Times*, July 8, 2017. www.nytimes.com/2017/07/08/us/he-became-a-hate-crime-victim-she-became-a-widow.html.

Dave Davies, "A Former Neo-Nazi Explains Why Hate Drew Him In—and How He Got Out," NPR, January 18, 2018. www.npr.org/2018/01/18/578745514/a-former-neo-nazi-explains-why-hate-drew-him-in-and-how-he-got-out.

Joe Heim, "Hate Groups in the US Remain on the Rise, According to New Study," *Washington Post*, February 21, 2018. www.washingtonpost.com/local/hate-groups-in-the-us-remain-on-the-rise-according-to-new-study/2018/02/21/6d28cbe0-1695-11e8-8b08-027a6ccb38eb_story.html?utm_term=.fd95718a0ba5.

Gretel Kauffman, "What Motivated Dylann Roof? Confession Offers Clues," *Christian Science Monitor*, December 11, 2016.

www.csmonitor.com/USA/2016/1211/What-motivated-Dylann-Roof-Confession-offers-clues.

German Lopez, "Why It's So Hard to Prosecute a Hate Crime," *Vox*, May 23, 2017. www.vox.com/identities/2017/4/10/15183902/hate-crime-trump-law.

Julie Moreau, "Growing Number of LGBTQ Candidates Seek Political Office in 2018," NBC News, January 29, 2018. www.nbcnews.com/feature/nbc-out/growing-number-lgbtq-candidates-seek-political-office-2018-n841961.

Erika Pesantes, "Stabbed for Being Black—a Hate Crime Victim Recalls Not Wanting to Die," *Orlando Sun-Sentinel*, December 31, 2017. www.sun-sentinel.com/local/broward/fl-sb-hate-crime-conviction-20171220-story.html.

Ken Schwencke, "Confusion, Fear, Cynicism: Why People Don't Report Hate Incidents," ProPublica, July 31, 2017. www.propublica.org/article/confusion-fear-cynicism-why-people-dont-report-hate-incidents.

Websites

FiveThirtyEight (https://fivethirtyeight.com). This website, maintained by well-known statistician Nate Silver, uses analytical data to explore many trends, including hate crimes. Among FiveThirtyEight's findings are that prior to the 2015 murders in Charleston, South Carolina's rate of hate crimes was well below the national average: the state ranked thirty-first in the number of hate crimes per million people.

Human Rights Campaign (www.hrc.org). In addition to other human rights topics, the campaign's website explores hate crimes committed against transgender people. The site provides statistics on crimes against transgender individuals as well as stories of crimes committed against members of the transgender community.

National Institute of Justice (NIJ) (www.nij.gov). An agency of the US Justice Department, the NIJ studies public policy issues and offers possible solutions. Among other issues, the NIJ's website explores the prevalence of hate crimes, the motivations behind the offenses, and how police should respond to hate crimes.

NPR: Stories About Hate Crimes (www.npr.org/tags/131511550/hate-crimes). NPR has assembled many stories about hate crimes, including coverage of the nine murders in Charleston, South Carolina, committed by Dylann Roof. Visitors can read transcripts of NPR stories on hate crimes and also listen to the broadcasts, which are archived on the site.

ProPublica (https://projects.propublica.org). A New York–based organization that conducts investigative journalism, ProPublica spent a year documenting hate crimes. The website's Documenting Hate project includes numerous stories written by ProPublica journalists. Victims of hate crimes or others who witnessed hate crimes are invited to submit their stories to the project.

San Francisco Police Department Special Investigations Division: Hate Crimes (https://sanfranciscopolice.org/special-investigations-div-hate-crimes). The San Francisco Police Department has tasked a team of detectives with the job of investigating hate crimes. Visitors to the hate crimes division website can download the report *Hate Crimes and the Victim*, which explains the rights of victims of hate crimes and how the city's police department responds to crimes of bias.

INDEX